Managing Library Technology

D1603390

LIBRARY INFORMATION TECHNOLOGY ASSOCIATION (LITA) GUIDES

Marta Mestrovic Deyrup, Ph.D.
Acquisitions Editor, Library Information and Technology Association,
a division of the American Library Association

The Library Information Technology Association (LITA) Guides provide information and guidance on topics related to cutting-edge technology for library and IT specialists.

Written by top professionals in the field of technology, the guides are sought after by librarians wishing to learn a new skill or to become current in today's best practices.

Each book in the series has been overseen editorially since conception by LITA and reviewed by LITA members with special expertise in the specialty area of the book.

Established in 1966, the Library and Information Technology Association (LITA) is the division of the American Library Association (ALA) that provides its members and the library and information science community as a whole with a forum for discussion, an environment for learning, and a program for actions on the design, development, and implementation of automated and technological systems in the library and information science field.

Approximately 25 LITA Guides were published by Neal-Schuman and ALA between 2007 and 2015. Rowman & Littlefield took over publication of the series beginning in late 2015. Books in the series published by Rowman & Littlefield are:

Digitizing Flat Media: Principles and Practices
The Librarian's Introduction to Programming Languages
Library Service Design: A LITA Guide to Holistic Assessment, Insight, and Improvement
Data Visualization: A Guide to Visual Storytelling for Librarians
Mobile Technologies in Libraries: A LITA Guide
Innovative LibGuides Applications
Integrating LibGuides into Library Websites
Protecting Patron Privacy: A LITA Guide
The LITA Leadership Guide: The Librarian as Entrepreneur, Leader, and Technologist
Using Social Media to Build Library Communities: A LITA Guide
Managing Library Technology: A LITA Guide

Managing Library Technology

A LITA Guide

Carson Block

ROWMAN & LITTLEFIELD
Lanham • Boulder • New York • London

Published by Rowman & Littlefield
A wholly owned subsidiary of The Rowman & Littlefield Publishing Group, Inc.
4501 Forbes Boulevard, Suite 200, Lanham, Maryland 20706
www.rowman.com

Unit A, Whitacre Mews, 26-34 Stannary Street, London SE11 4AB

British Library Cataloguing in Publication Information Available

Library of Congress Cataloging-in-Publication Data Available

ISBN 9781442271807 (hardback : alk. paper) | ISBN 9781442271814 (pbk. : alk. paper) | ISBN
9781442271821 (ebook)

∞ ™ The paper used in this publication meets the minimum requirements of American
National Standard for Information Sciences Permanence of Paper for Printed Library
Materials, ANSI/NISO Z39.48-1992.

Printed in the United States of America

Contents

Preface

MANAGEMENT OF TECHNOLOGY

Management of technology has become one of the more daunting issues facing library workers of all stripes. How does one manage something so unruly—so unpredictable—and always so much in motion? For many libraries, especially small to midsize, the tasks involved in taming the technological beast are also among the most challenging and often intimidating efforts faced by library workers. This is true even for large libraries and library systems—no matter the size of the library, technology can be tough. And where are library workers to turn to learn more about managing technology? Recent graduates of schools teaching library information science tell me that technology is rarely—if ever—covered as part of the curriculum. Fortunately, there are many (often free) opportunities to learn about specific technologies or initiatives, but few (if any) covering the broad concepts that help library people make good decisions and actions with their technological efforts. I'm here to bring you good news: not only can a non-technologist understand the basics of technology management, but the concepts can be harnessed to help you and your library thrive!

Managing Library Technology: A LITA Guide aims to highlight the enduring elements of technology management—the things that stay the same regardless of ongoing changes, trends, and other actions that make up our modern technological "churn." Whether you are a library director, an "accidental technologist," or—as indicated by the experiences of those taking the ALA-APA Certified Public Library Administrator (CPLA) class I teach—even someone with a great deal of experience in managing technology in libraries, there are likely concepts here that will make a difference in how you approach technology in your library. Shared in plain language and in a down-to-earth manner, you'll learn what makes technology tick. You'll gain the planning and management tools to harness its full force to bring essential support and boundless possibilities to your organization.

AN OVERVIEW OF THE TOPICS IN THIS BOOK

Throughout *Managing Library Technology: A LITA Guide*, we'll take a comfortably paced look at what it takes to enjoy successful technology efforts in your library, with the aim of giving you a deeper understanding of the role of technology in your library and a mastery of the important issues.

In chapter 1, we'll explore some of the broad topics that help us understand the context of technology and how it all fits into the bigger picture, considering things like your own vision for technology, the technology market (and how the library fits into the greater ecosystem), integrating technology into existing plans and efforts, a first-blush look at technology budgets in libraries, why technology policy is important to every library, and more. By bridging the concepts of technology vision, market forces, patron desires, and staff needs, you'll see your own pathways to connect library goals with technological possibilities.

Chapter 2 contains a brief but powerful look at performing a basic technology assessment, with the purpose of becoming familiar with the library's current technological environment.

In chapters 3 and 4, we will dive deep into the process of technology planning. Many of us know the folly of strict plans (the future, after all, is often unpredictable), but we also know that the planning process has enormous value as a way to help us identify our big goals and think through and anticipate how we might tackle them. As President Dwight D. Eisenhower once said: "Plans are worthless, but planning is everything." In these chapters, we'll embrace the spirit and identify the mechanics of the planning process.

In chapter 5, we'll increase our understanding of the nuts and bolts of technology implementation and in the process learn how to stay agile in an ever-changing environment. As in chapter 1, here we will learn concepts that help us understand the context of technology implementation and strategies to make wise choices. You'll connect your technology implementation efforts with who you serve—drawing a straight line between efforts and impacts.

Chapter 6 is dedicated to evaluation of technology. In other words, how are we doing? How do we know? Have our efforts been effective? If not, how can we modify our course to get back on track?

In chapter 7, we'll "put it all together" and consider some of the constant elements within our ever-changing technological landscape. You'll learn about the role and impacts of emerging technologies affecting library services and how to factor that change into your own approach and walk away with confidence in this little-understood and increasingly important area of library operations.

In my ALA-APA CPLA Management of Technology class, students are given current templates, spreadsheets, and forms to help them practice essential technology management concepts. Throughout this book, I share examples of those tools so that you can build your own! The tools include methods to capture and record technology budgets, tally technology resources, organize brainstorming sessions, create process diagrams, and more.

Not only is it possible to tame the technological beast in the library, but I believe library workers of all stripes, levels, and abilities can harness the power of what can be called "applied magic" to benefit patrons, empower staff, and help the library thrive! I believe readers will find the concepts in *Managing Library Technology: A LITA Guide* simple to understand and applicable in areas well beyond computers and digital systems. Are you ready to get a handle on the pieces and parts that make up the technology effort in your library and harness them for the benefit of not just your community but also your sanity? Good—let's begin!

Acknowledgments

To library consultant Pat Wagner, who suggested that the fundamentals of technology management were not widely known in libraries and that I should take the time to do something about it.

To instructional designer Alese Smith, who helped me translate my career experience into the lessons that form the basis of this book.

To the many library workers across the country who have helped hone this material through their participation in my ALA-APA Certified Public Library Administrator online class Management of Technology and to the next generation of students.

Chapter One

Introduction to Library Technology

In many libraries, the world of technology has been shrouded in mystery, complete with strange denizens, exotic rituals, and a vocabulary that is often incomprehensible to a layperson. This world is also a place of wonder, where some libraries—those in the know—have fulfilled the needs of patrons and their communities in new and exciting ways. In truth, technology is an institutional asset and as essential to delivering library services as physical facilities. All too often, though, opportunities are missed simply because librarians don't understand the basics of what technology can do and how it can further the goals of the library.

Technology doesn't have to be difficult to understand. In my experience (and I believe in the experience of many library technologists), almost anyone, despite where they might fall on the "geek" scale, can grasp the fundamental principles behind most of the technology used in libraries. This chapter sets the broad context for technology to help remove any mysteries in a manner that uses timeless principles as a basis to understand, manage, and prosper in an ever-changing world.

In chapter 1, contextual topics include:

- examining our own orientation to library technology

- technology vision and the big picture
- proactive vs. reactive approaches to technology
- the cart and the horse
- computer platforms: faith and agnosticism
- how library technology fits into the greater technological ecosystem
- a first look at the library technology budget
- saving money with technology?
- the role of learning
- your new best friend—the whiteboard
- the impact of technology policy on library operations
- tying technology into existing library efforts and plans

It might be helpful to think of this chapter as a variety bowl of "fun size" candy bars—little bite-size chunks that give an idea of what each of their bigger versions look and taste like. Some readers might already understand these concepts (and can skim right through), but I've found that sharing some of these basic concepts helps illuminate some aspects of tech that aren't always understood outside of the world of IT.

EXAMINING OUR OWN ORIENTATION TO TECHNOLOGY

To best understand technology, it's helpful to first examine one's own attitude toward it. Technology adoption in libraries is uneven—some have embraced changes, while others have only come along under silent (and sometimes not-so-silent) protest. Even though technology is a given (a modern library cannot function without tech), there are still some library workers who wish this tech thing would just go away. On the other hand, we have many others who are positioning their library on the bleeding edge of technology. In the middle is a gap of understanding and adoption of tech. In the places where this gap exists, I've found that the source is not having a shared knowledge among staff of how the role of technology has impacted and changed libraries.

In the recent past, the library's content focus was mostly on materials (primarily books) that are static—they didn't change much over time. My favorite example of this is the "ready reference" collection found behind most reference desks; even though updated editions of these materials were purchased every year, the content didn't change very much, and many reference librarians could rely on nothing more than muscle memory to locate the needed chapter and verse in these tomes. Communications channels, too, were much simpler—mostly limited to one person, the telephone, and sometimes memos and letters.

Today, materials are increasingly active and electronic; not only are they subject to constant change, but sometimes the location of the information changes too (so much for muscle memory). Static resources are still useful, but the real action is to be found in the dynamic nature of electronic resources. As well as what we previously considered as credible sources of information, phenomena like social media have given new perspectives on breaking news events, expert opinion on obscure topics, and more. And the number of communications channels that technology has made possible continues to be mind-boggling. Clearly, Alvin Toffler (author of the seminal 1970 book *Future Shock*) was on to something when he said, "The illiterate of the 21st century will not be those who cannot read and write, but those who cannot learn, unlearn and relearn."

Understanding your own feelings about technology is a great place to start. Some love tech while others don't. Regardless, technology is here to stay. Library workers don't need to love technology, but they do need to master it as an essential resource and tool and, in the right cases, a turbo-boost in serving patrons and communities.

TECHNOLOGY VISION AND THE BIG PICTURE

Technology in libraries often appears more complex than it really is. Like most things, the key is to first understand what you want to accomplish and then determine how technology can (or should) assist you in meeting goals. This concept is simple, the perception that it's a complex topic has sometimes interfered with what is probably the most powerful driving technology force in a library: the vision for how to use technology to serve communities.

Due to ongoing change in the tech world, technology in libraries can take on a mysterious air. It makes sense—all media undergoes specialization as it evolves. In human history, nothing has specialized as quickly as the Internet and the technologies that power it, and perhaps no other area of library service has evolved as quickly, visibly, and spectacularly as technology. Stating the obvious, keeping track of it all is impossible and can be intimidating. Tracking changes can be made simpler, though. Those of us who make our living in technology simply focus on the topics that interest us the most and enjoy teaming with others with different and complementary expertise. It's not just a feel-good technique but an absolute survival strategy. The topics, too, tend to evolve or change over time—sometimes many times within a single day.

Some librarians I've worked with say that they don't have a particular vision when it comes to technology, saying instead things like "I just want it to work" (well, me too!) and "The vision for technology has to come from somewhere else in the library—I just don't understand it." Technology is a prime and growing resource to help libraries serve patrons—so please allow me to say that it's not OK to forgo at least a sense of how you want to use it as a resource.

Stating the vision does not have to be hard—and I'm not suggesting that anyone undergo the often-painful process of creating a single vision "statement." Identifying goals in a clear enough manner—clear enough to write down using just a few sentences or even a bulleted list—is a great start. Many people find that once they articulate their thoughts—almost like magic—solutions will suggest themselves from the wide range of options and approaches available. This is the power of connecting your unspoken vision with the rigidity of words on a page (or whiteboard—more on that later).

It's true that technology can suggest certain goals or make previously impossible goals attainable, but be careful. More on that topic later in this chapter ("The Cart and the Horse").

Like most things in life, there are multiple ways to accomplish a particular objective. In my experience (as a worker, IT manager/director, and consultant), I've found that I'm most successful when I concentrate more on the *objectives and outcomes* required of efforts and projects than on the exact path that I or others may choose to perform and accomplish them. We often get hung up on the "how" and can quickly lose sight of our ultimate objective or outcome. This trap certainly shows up in other areas of our lives as leaders and managers, but in technology, it can be downright deadly.

In truth—and especially in technology—there are often multiple acceptable "hows" to accomplish a particular goal or outcome. Naturally, people tend to play to their strengths, and when a technologist has experienced a great deal of success using a particular technology, they can sometimes begin to mistakenly think it's the only "how" that really works. That thinking is generally flawed and has led to bad experiences for many in libraries. More on that subject in a bit.

PROACTIVE VS. REACTIVE APPROACHES TO TECHNOLOGY

There tends to be two distinct approaches favored by IT professionals: proactive and reactive.

Proactive folks are the ones who look ahead. Planners at heart, they are typified by the old carpenter's expression "Measure twice, cut once." Proactive techs are most often found among those who look after networks and servers.

Reactive folks are usually quick thinkers and are equally quick to action. They love the heat of battle and often say, "Let's try it and see what happens." Reactive techs are most often found among the people providing desktop and help-desk support.

Librarians need to be both proactive and reactive. The trick, then, is in balance. Ideally, you have both approaches on your IT team—whether through a complementary mix of individuals or through a single person who has the skills to employ both approaches at the right times.

If you are the one tasked with technology support for your library, the next time you're addressing a tech issue ask yourself, "Is this a time to be reactive or proactive?" For the less experienced, the reactive response is the one that can often jump the lead, but it's not always the right choice.

THE CART AND THE HORSE   *goal specified BEFORE action*

The cart and the horse. The tail and the dog. In the proper orientation, mighty efforts can be accomplished (and if the wagging tail is any indication, even enjoyed). Putting these elements in the right order is simple, and it can be done every time.

Among technologists, especially those adept at project planning, you'll often hear this concept applied in terms of "drivers" as used in the question "What elements are driving our efforts in this area?" Or more simply "What are our drivers?"

Drivers can be a bit of a confusing term because it can apply to a spectrum of elements, including a description of the desired technological "thing" or outcome of a tech project, plans (formal and informal), desires, and other factors. To avoid any confusion, I often think of drivers as the most important elements influencing my decisions and actions. Drivers are kind of like the action-hero cousins of "objectives."

"But what about constraints, like not enough budget or time? Aren't those drivers too?" Technically, yes, but I encourage waiting a bit before factoring in possible constraints. I think the most important aspect is first identifying what should be accomplished—often stated as a goal, outcome, or impact. Once a target is established, then it's time to consider the resources needed to achieve it, the obstacles to overcome, and the time needed to make it happen.

Too often, actions are taken—especially complex or expensive actions—without first articulating the intended goals, the desired outcomes, or the preferred impacts of the efforts. The path to create the proper orientation between the cart and the horse starts with a question considered earlier in this chapter—what do we want to accomplish? If you do a good job with this first step, your entire effort will benefit. First identifying your goals, outcomes, or impacts is the key to success in technology projects and ongoing efforts.

As you go through the process, especially when things get confusing, you'll refer back to your goals, outcomes, or impacts to see if you're on track. Upon examination, it's always possible that you might need to change tracks (by modifying your objectives or tasks), but that should always be a conscious decision and one evident to all involved in the applicable effort.

COMPUTER PLATFORMS—FAITH AND AGNOSTICISM

Many of us are passionate about our computers and the digital services we use through them. In an age when computing devices are becoming smaller, more powerful, and even fashionable, that passion has become more pronounced.

Technologists who use and manage computers to make their living can be even more passionate. Depending on their personal and professional experiences, through trial and error, and, hopefully, through a track record of success, many have formed strong opinions on the one "correct" path to accomplish a particular technological effort and are faithful to their beliefs.

There's a downfall to this approach. Such beliefs can border on religious fervor, and these passionate, platform-devoted people are (sometimes unfairly but often comically) referred to in a derogatory fashion: Apple fanboys or fangirls, Unix zealots, "Windoze" tools, and other inflammatory names from others who are just as passionate about their own biases.

Just as to a hammer, every problem looks like a nail, techs with strong platform orientations will tend to look at every computing effort in terms of only what is capable through their platform of choice. In the old days (the early 1990s), this was a good bet (captured in the phrase "no one ever got fired for buying IBM") but is increasingly risky as computing and communications increasingly specialize, combine, split, and change. Locking ourselves into a single platform or vendor approach is increasingly becoming problematic, if not dangerous. In terms of technology, diversity tends to keep us safer and more agile than a monoculture. On the challenging side, there are costs (including time, effort, and money) associated with a diverse computing environment. It's certainly a more difficult path, but I believe the right one.

I often describe myself as "platform agnostic." Although I don't know for sure that a true technology nirvana exists, I do believe this: there are many paths on the road to heavenly computing experiences, and the more options I allow myself to consider, the better the final outcomes. Amen!

HOW DOES LIBRARY TECHNOLOGY FIT INTO THE GREATER TECHNOLOGICAL ECOSYSTEM?

ILS (Follet? WCSD)

The Integrated Library System (ILS) is not only the most expensive; it is arguably the library's most important technology platform. It is the core system responsible for supporting the major business operations of the library. The ILS helps us keep track of patrons and physical materials; it enables us to circulate real and virtual items; it supports our workflows in acquiring and cataloging new materials; and more. The success of a library is dependent on an ILS that performs these core business functions in a manner that is at least satisfactory, if not close to perfect.

Of course, a system of this importance comes with a significant price—and often sticker shock. Considering what it takes to purchase an ILS and migrate holdings into the new system, and the addition of ongoing costs such as annual subscriptions, support fees, and staffing costs, you might begrudgingly feel like you're personally driving the library technology market with your substantial investment.

Why are ILSs so expensive? Consider for a moment its uniqueness in the world of technology. The ILS is kind of like a combination of some other off-the-shelf systems (including inventory systems, purchasing systems, customer relations management or CRM systems, web servers, self-service kiosks, and others) but not exactly like any of those systems. No other market—other than libraries—needs an ILS. In short, the ILS is a special system in a very small market.

As large as some of our costs seem, what libraries pay for tech is just a drop in the bucket when compared to other technology-centric industries (and indeed, libraries are increasingly becoming technology-centric organizations). The lion's share of most library *Budget* budgets is devoted to staffing costs, materials (our "inventory"), and buildings—in other industries, tech expenditures are much more prominent. For example, companies offering ride-sharing services (such as Uber and Lyft) have few actual employees (drivers are "contractors") and hardly any inventory or property (the "contractors" are driving their own cars, after all), but as a software company, you can bet they continually double-down on technology expenses.

The library technology market is tiny compared to the overall volume of commerce in the tech sector. Even with all our technology expenditures—and including my assertion that libraries are becoming increasingly technology-centric—in the scope of things, we're really what's considered a niche market. That means we're really not driving too much when it comes to the larger tech world and are often in the back seat on this wild ride. This plays out in several areas, including the specific functions technology can perform for us, the availability and development of new applicable technologies, and cost.

Part of the dilemma in being a niche market is that libraries rightfully have high expectations of the technology capabilities that we want but are often unaware that developing those capabilities requires a significant amount of dollars, people, time, and other resources—often much more than most libraries are able or willing to devote. For a small market, libraries are a tough crowd to please—we rightfully want our systems to be as responsive to us as we are to our patrons but often don't understand what it takes for us or our vendors to get there, and we rarely have the cash to invest to make things happen.

A common complaint I hear is that some of our specialized systems (certainly the ILS, but also packages that help us manage public computers, printing, our online services, and other areas) have fewer features or are more "buggy" than their counterparts in the commercial world. Are some of these complaints valid? Well, yes. But before getting too irritated, it's helpful to understand the environment. Again, let's consider the ILS.

tech probs w/ILS *(handwritten annotation)*

open-source software *(handwritten annotation)*

ILSs were created in a special way—with vendors building nascent systems around the needs of a single large customer and then attempting to adapt that system for other libraries over time. This has resulted in modern ILSs that have strengths in some areas and weaknesses in others. Unfortunately, in the ILS paradigm, we don't have the option of just using what we feel works best—"integrated" most often means "take it or leave it."

This environment results in some of the tensions between libraries and their technology vendors. Vendors have a substantial investment in their systems, and we as customers are often entrenched in our own processes and how they interact with our systems. In short, it's not that easy for vendors or libraries to change, even when we all want to. Thankfully, for those willing to roll up their sleeves, open-source software—which literally allows libraries to take their technology destinies into their own hands—is an option to explore (with eyes wide open—open source is free as in "freedom" and not free as in "beer"). We'll talk about open source more in a future chapter.

For some of us library technologists, it's apparent that the core approach—the idea of a single platform that "integrates" all of the library's business functions—is an outdated notion. Modern technology services outside of libraries are increasingly built from a mix—combining dedicated systems that have been designed from the ground up to inter-operate with other dedicated systems that allow a customer of technology to "mix and match" these dedicated systems to serve their needs. While mixing these systems certainly requires expertise, testing, and plain hard work, the reward is agile technology services that are not dependent on the strengths and weaknesses of a single vendor.

Although I feel some vendors could do more to modernize their approaches, I also think we need to give vendors a break. Although I'm not in love with the "Integrated" part of the ILS, and am aware that through mergers and acquisitions our number of ILS vendors is shrinking (making the market less competitive), I'm grateful that we have good vendors invested in serving our smaller and specialized library market. The next time you're working with a vendor of library-specific technology, especially if you're frustrated by something they can't do for you, consider for a moment the smaller scale of the market they're serving. There's a magnitude of difference in the depth, breadth, and resources of a company that provides Radio Frequency Identification (RFID) systems for the Walmarts of the world and one concentrating on the library market.

A FIRST LOOK AT THE LIBRARY TECHNOLOGY BUDGET (ACTIVITY)

It's time to move from theoretical to the practical for a moment and get an idea of how the library is currently resourcing its budget to provide for technology needs. To perform this exercise, locate copies of your annual budget. A higher-level overview is fine, and this exercise will work best if you can locate three to five years of your budgets.

Using pen and paper—or a software tool like a spreadsheet program—create two simple grids that look something like this:

1. Record your main technology lines in the top row. The middle row is for any obvious technology expenses you may have that didn't show up in your main technology line. Look around your budget document—you may be surprised!
2. Add the two to come up with the total for each year.

Table 1.1.   Simple Budget Grid—Total Library Budget

	Year 1	Year 2	Year 3	Year 4	This Year	Next Year
Total Library Budget						

This is where you record your bottom-line figure.

Table 1.2. Simple Budget Grid—Technology Budget

	Year 1	Year 2	Year 3	Year 4	This Year	Next Year
Main Technology Lines						
Extras						
Total						

Through this process, you're refreshing your memory on what you currently spend on library technology.

1. Compare the bottom lines on the columns.
2. Consider the correlations between your overall budget and your technology expenses each year.
3. Start spotting your trends.

Intrigued? Don't stop here! Grab more granular data if you wish and do the same sort of comparisons.

SAVING MONEY WITH TECHNOLOGY?

Relatively speaking—considering other library expenses—technology is expensive. And despite my cavalier response to the question, the truth is that you can save money with technology—but in libraries it's often indirect, through efficiencies that technology can provide in other areas. In other IT-driven professions, a concept called "economy of scale" is realized directly by taking advantage of how easily some technologies can scale up—i.e., easily and inexpensively grow—without a significant increase in expenses. In this sort of economy of scale, as the number of technology users increases, the cost of serving each user decreases. It's a neat trick, but it doesn't easily apply to libraries because priorities for most libraries are rightfully driven by the people directly served. That means libraries do lots of things that don't easily scale beyond local services, and technology certainly fits into that category.

Let's use Radio Frequency Identification (RFID) as one example. The up-front costs, in terms of dollars and staff time, are significant. Even with the cost of library RFID tags dropping over time (remember—libraries are not a major influence in the technology market), the per-tag cost is a significant factor, as are the other components of the system. The effort to tag items is a major endeavor (every item needs to be touched and processed by human hands). A move to RFID represents a significant investment.

The efficiency gains from migrating to RFID can be equally significant. One common rationale to convert to RFID is to greatly improve efficiencies in your circulation department, and if your circulation department needs help, RFID could be your magic bullet. But even if your circulation department is already efficient, RFID can still have significant impacts by greatly improving customer service and the overall patron experience. When combined with self-check systems, e-commerce at the terminal, and other services, it can go even farther. In certain cases, the investment in RFID can, over time, pay for itself in terms of the efficiencies it can bring to your customer service efforts.

So yes, to my chagrin, technology can really save you money. The biggest gains often come indirectly and often through efficiencies.

THE ROLE OF LEARNING

The library's investment in technology is substantial. To get the most out of this investment, we need to understand the capabilities of what we have and how to squeeze every last drop of functionality out of our technology systems. The path, of course, is learning—which we sometimes think of only as "training," but there are many ways to gain knowledge.

We don't ever really buy technology—but only rent its capabilities for a certain time period. Specific technologies have a lifespan of usefulness—most of the digital systems that we use in libraries have a fairly short time cycle (i.e., we try to replace PCs ever three to five years; new versions of operating systems and major systems are frequently released, etc.). The actual time frame varies, but as the old blues song goes: "When it all comes down, you've got to go back to mother earth." One way to make the best use of the useful period of any technology is to commit the time it takes to learn as much as possible about the outcomes that you need from your technology and the techniques to achieve those outcomes and use that knowledge to get the most out of your systems.

Since technology is expensive and only useful for a certain time period, not getting the most from it by providing for learning (via training or other means) is akin to throwing money out in the street. ^[integrate] Learning comes in many forms—in person, classroom, online, self-paced, peer-to-peer, through organizational culture, and more. How ^[training tech into plan] you go about training can vary and should reflect what works best for your institutions—just remember to include it as part of your approach! So often libraries deploy new technology without much advanced learning and try to "wing it," resulting in unintended consequences, including poor performance from the technology itself and a generally negative attitude toward tech.

In tight budget times, training is one of the first lines to be targeted. I've always challenged that notion—today there are more learning options than ever, and while all learning requires an investment of time, the actual costs can be in the no-to-low category. ^[low cost training] One excellent method is simply getting together with others on a regular basis to talk about technology topics. Such gatherings help each participant learn new things on the spot and also spur more research.

IT professionals are always learning. Given the rate of change in tech, it's a core strategy that you should have as well.

THE WHITEBOARD

Although techs are a notoriously independent bunch, proud of their unique outlooks and approaches, there is one thing most of us have in common: the whiteboard.

Oh, in a pinch, chart paper and markers can do, and blank paper and a pencil (with a good eraser) are almost as good. But a large erasable surface (and markers—especially a variety of colors) is one of the most powerful ways to check one's own logic and understanding, troubleshoot, build ideas as individuals or teams, and communicate those ideas during the present and into the future.

This simple "chalk and slate" approach is very powerful. Although what we do with technology can be visionary and fanciful, the process of designing a technology solution, mapping a process and timeline, and other supporting factors tends to follow a more rational and logical flow. Committing the ideas to the board in a linear fashion helps us do a good job by allowing us and others to test our ideas and assumptions and ultimately make good decisions.

Of course, the whiteboard is literally a blank slate and can be used for many other purposes, including fanciful daydreaming and mind mapping. One of my favorite applications is seen in restaurants where artists can use the same tools to create beautiful works of art. What's not to love about the whiteboard?

And another reason I call the whiteboard a best friend? I often take pictures of each beautiful one before erasing it for the next idea or project. If not a best friend, why else would I continue to take snapshots?

TECHNOLOGY POLICY

What does technology policy have to do with running a library?

With so much of our efforts being supported or driven by technology, technology policy has emerged as very important to libraries. If you haven't been paying attention, now is a great time to start. You can get a jumpstart through our professional organizations, including the American Library Association's Office of Information Technology Policy (OITP). ALA's OITP tracks many national issues relevant to libraries.

There are many other sources in our field, including organizations like your state library or your local library association's legislative committee.

I also recommend looking outside of our field to follow those who are following the big picture. Issues like digital rights management, telecommunications tariffs, the Universal Service Fund (better known to libraries as E-Rate), net neutrality, copyright, broadband access, wireless availability, and more are vitally important.

These issues are also big business, ensuring that a number of information sources, including business publications, are also keeping a close eye. I read lots of tech blogs, but one of my favorite sources of information for current technology events affecting a broad subsection of society is the good ol' *Wall Street Journal*.

If technology policy isn't a compelling interest to you, find a staff member, colleague, or friend to whom it is. Meet with them as often as necessary (over breakfast, lunch, coffee, or other beverages) and stay fluent in the issues as they emerge.

TYING TECH INTO EXISTING LIBRARY EFFORTS AND PLANS

Modern libraries can seem tossed about by changes in the technology landscape (including electronic content, new communications technologies, statistics, and more), but our institutional missions tend to have a different focus (including education, enlightenment, community service, and more) where the technology piece acts in a supporting role. Ideally, the role of technology is to first support those institutional missions, as well as to suggest new approaches and opportunities.

Some technologies are so seductive that we can easily get confused. These can be so great that instead of simply seeing how they can help support our missions, we re-form our missions around their capabilities. That can sometimes be a good idea, but you have to first have a very deep understanding of the technology and evaluate how close it is to your primary goals.

We can put this concept into play. Think for a moment about library websites that you use—your own and others. It's likely that the sites are emulating a successful style that already exists, either among libraries or elsewhere. Study the home page. Explore the most prominent links or features. Do you feel that style reflects the objectives of the specific library? Why or why not?

An example: when it comes to emulating a technological look and feel, for many years, Google has remained a favorite. Google (and its many offerings) is certainly attractive because the visible product is clean, fast, and simple. While it's true that creating a great search engine was Google's initial goal, these days it seems that Google's primary objective is data mining. The company today offers a very wide range of products and services and is in the business of monitoring how we use its products to do a better job at generating revenue through advertising and other means—as well as improving those services to keep us all coming back for more.

So, when we say we want to be more like Google, do we mean we want a quick and simple interface or a business model that focuses each effort on ultimately generating more revenue? Do libraries and Google share the same objectives?

Asking questions like these when considering our own technological objectives can be very helpful in honing in on the key things we're inspired by—and may want to emulate—and as a way of identifying things that really aren't aligned with what we're trying to accomplish. This exercise is the basis of determining what is worth chasing—and what should be left alone.

vendors

Vendors can add to the confusion by putting together great packages of dissimilar technologies, including the one you asked for bundled with one or ones you didn't know you "needed." One example comes from our personal lives: cable television. If you are a cable subscriber, how many channels are available to you versus how many you actually watch?

Beware of these library tech bundles. If you know your institutional objectives, you will also know if these packages will really work for you. If not, they have the possible consequence of steering you away from where you would really like to go—and at the very least adding unnecessary work to what is probably your already overallocated schedule.

How do we keep all this straight? One way might be though the use of that whiteboard I wrote about earlier in this chapter. Using a few, simple words, write down the major things you're trying to achieve with your technology efforts. When considering "bundles," ask the questions such as:

what are you trying to achieve w/ technology?

- Will this get us there?
- Does this take us in the opposite direction?
- Are there other ways to get us there?

The work of documenting your goals and objectives may have already been performed. Be sure to keep any written plans handy, including library long-range plans and certainly your technology plan (which we will learn about in a future chapter). Periodically review these plans with others, and make the relevance of a particular technology part of your discussions.

Here are a few areas to explore:

- What official or unofficial strategic plans and efforts exist?
- What vision does library leadership have for technology?

- Is there a shared understanding of the role of technology in the library—including you, your board, your staff, your community, and others?

Chapter Two

Basic Technology Assessment

Before digging into the process of determining technology destiny (through technology planning—covered in the next chapters), it's important to keep feet firmly planted in the present—with a few shuffle-steps back into the past—to understand the current state of the library and its technology efforts.

I like to place an emphasis on thoughtful assessment—essentially checking in on the current state of everything that contributes to the library's technology efforts and operations and recording the results to use as a basis for planning. This process offers the opportunity to not just observe and collect information, but also presents a chance to think about the library's existing resources and how they are currently managed. It's an excellent set of warm-up activities for the technology planning process!

It's time to get familiar with the library's technological environment. The topics in this brief chapter are designed to help paint a clear picture of the current state of the library's technology in order to start on a firm foundation. Chapter 2 topics include:

- assessing the big picture
- looking closely at technology systems, people, and the technology budget

• reflecting and discussing the number to find true meaning

ASSESSMENT — THE BIG PICTURE

I've found that simple technology assessment activities can get a short shrift in libraries. Many feel like they know already know what they have and view assessment as somehow "getting in the way" of action. That is, of course, until they start digging in a little and start making surprising discoveries. A good assessment equals a good start!

A simple test of a person's understanding of a particular topic is to ask them to teach others about it. Can they explain the key concepts clearly and simply in a way that others can understand? I suggest applying the same concept to understanding the library technology environment. In the process of collecting details about the process, key concepts are sure to emerge (things such as "I thought we had better WiFi coverage!" or "People really hate our Internet computers!"). A good assessment will help capture raw numbers and help summarize, in simple terms, the current state of the library's technology efforts and provide a launch platform for future improvements.

Library technology assessments start with taking an inventory and typically identify:

• Who is served by the technology?
• What are the current services and service levels?
• What technology resources does the library currently have—and what resources are desirable?
• What sort of human resources—i.e., staff—are devoted to technology?
• What infrastructures are used to deliver technology to staff and users?

Each library is a little different in terms of taking inventory. Below are some questions to start the process—not just noting what the library has but also the quantities of each.

Who Is Served?

Libraries exist to serve the needs of people, so identifying the people to a degree of specificity is helpful. All libraries serve patrons of some sort—what types of patrons are served by the library? Children? Parents? Teens? Adults? Students? Seniors? Businesses? Specialty groups—like lawyers, government agencies, researchers, and more? Others? If many different groups are served, are there particular ones receiving more focus than others?

Libraries also serve the needs of staff with technology. What technology tools do staff need to do their jobs? What tools are missing?

Are there any special populations within these groups? Different ethnicities with different communication needs? Disabled? Under-served populations? Others?

What Services Are Offered?

What services are currently delivered to library patrons using technology?

Most libraries already have a website. What information and services are offered? Access to holdings? General information? Patron accounts allowing folks to renew items, place holds, and more? Participation in consortiums? E-commerce for fines and fees? Subscription databases? Access to historic collections? Discovery interfaces or tools? Links to social media sites? Others?

What in-house technologies are offered? Computers to access the Internet and library catalog? Accessible workstations? A computer training lab or labs? Digital creation stations? Scanners and copiers? Others?

Technology Systems, Devices, and People Inventory

Most libraries have or have access to an Integrated Library System (ILS) and have computers and other technology devices for patrons and staff. Does the library have a Makerspace? Is there staff dedicated to technology needs? Are there contracts for services or other forms of outsourcing? Does the library have its own servers? Network infrastructure? Wireless systems? Mobile phones or other mobile devices? Software licensing agreements? Other items?

What Is Desired?

What current technological developments excite the community, library staff, director, library board, and others? What have staff seen that could improve services for patrons or boost efficiencies or comfort for staff? What sorts of things that don't yet exist might library staff want to invent?

What Else?

What has been missed by the questions above?

A CLOSER LOOK AT EXISTING RESOURCES

It's time to put a real or virtual pen to paper and do some actual counting!

There are a couple of ways to count—it can be as simple as just taking a look around or (in the case of technology components) using helpers like electronic inventory tools that can automate the process. This nuts-and-bolts process is an important starting point.

- If the library has an IT department, it might already use any tools that count things electronically. If the library participated in a technology grant in the past, it might have used an electronic inventory tool that they provided. These electronic tools only count devices connected to the network.

- If the library doesn't have such a tool, it's okay. Counting the good old-fashioned way—by walking around and making hash marks—is perfectly acceptable.
- Use tally sheets to take some basic counts of computer resources, including computers, network infrastructure, and software.

A Closer Look at the ILS

The ILS (Integrated Library System) is arguably the biggest and most important technology resource the library possesses. "Integrated" means that the most important functions—including cataloging, circulation, acquisitions, the electronic "card catalog," many library websites, and other functions—are managed by a single computer system.

While it's true that the network is almost as important (without access via a good network, the best ILS in the world is useless), the ILS is special to library operations. It is fed with data about materials and other resources in our collections and information about patrons, and it is used to locate materials in-house, circulate materials on loan, levy and collect fines, place items on hold, and many other work processes. Simply put, most of us live or die on our ILS.

How well is your ILS working for you? It's a best practice to evaluate the performance of the ILS every once in a while (perhaps every five years or so), look at the market to see what options exist, and consider whether the current choice is still the best choice.

Since the ILS is so fundamental to library operations, it's taken for granted in some libraries that changing to a new system is unlikely. Or perhaps some fear what might happen if the library migrates to a new one. I would like to encourage every library to not take the ILS for granted—but instead make regular evaluation part of the library's life cycle. Each library is probably quite different today than the day each started with its current ILS, and it's possible that the library's needs could be better served with a different approach—or the library may discover you're in a perfect position. Without a periodic look, it's hard to tell.

Not sure where to start?
Library Technology Guides: http://librarytechnology.org/
Marshall Breeding, former director for innovative technologies and research at the Jean and Alexander Heard Library at Vanderbilt University, publishes an essential guide for those following what is arguably the most important (and expensive) electronic resource in libraries: the Integrated Library System, or ILS. Marshall's site contains vital statistics on market share of ILS systems across the globe, a graphical chart showing the history of mergers and acquisitions in the ILS, current news about the ILS market, and more. Marshall's historical perspective is a key strategic tool when considering one of the library's greatest resources.

TECHNOLOGY BUDGET – A CLOSER LOOK

In chapter 1, I suggested taking a very broad look at library technology expenses, and I hinted that perhaps some libraries are spending money for technology in some areas without realizing it. Upon closer examination, many libraries discover that they are devoting more of their budgets in technology expenditures than earlier realized.

Why? Because over time technology has snuck into almost everything libraries do, and like a thief in the night, it entered some areas without much notice—and then took over.

To get a clearer picture, many perform a tech-centric financial inventory. Time to pull out the library's annual budget again, but this time it should be reviewed with whoever helps prepare the library budget—the finance officer, IT manager, an accountant, or other professional. Budgets are constructed in various ways, so here's one approach to taking a financial inventory:

- Any existing budget lines for technology expenses are an excellent starting point. Some libraries already have detailed budget lines and subledgers devoted to areas of technology expenses. I've discovered that a surprising number of libraries do not have discrete budget lines for technology or have spread technology expenses throughout their budget documents, making it difficult to gauge actual expenses.
- Start with whatever detailed information exists, carefully considering exactly what that budget pays for. If it's not clear what the budget lines fund, talk to the finance and/or IT manager. Make notes to help keep track with a goal of clear understanding what the technology budget is going toward.
- Next, look at the collection. Does the library offer electronic resources? While most accurately considered a collection expense, some libraries consider it a technology expense (since the format of the information is electronic). Consider collection-related expenses not already accounted for in the technology line. Does the library have self-check units? Theft prevention systems? RFID?
- If not already accounted for in the tech budget, Internet access and e-mail systems are certainly a tech expense.
- Materials processing functions, whether in-sourced through the library's own technical services department or outsourced, involve a great number of technology expenses.
- Does the library use an automated materials handling system?
- Now look at "back office" functions—the sorts of things that occur, for instance, in administrative spaces, for expenses such as telephones and mobile devices. Does the library use electronic systems for time cards, human resources, accounting, ordering, or other functions?

PEOPLE — A CLOSER LOOK

As with other parts of the library, the most expensive—and arguably most important—resource is the people who make things run. Since technology is so good at automating mundane processes, counting and measuring things for us, and more, it's easy to overlook the fact that we still need good old human oversight to make the best decisions on how to run the systems.

Since good implementation of technology goes hand in hand with efficiencies, many IT shops are also models of efficiency, requiring just a few folks to manage a large number of machines and services. It's also easy to take these human resources for granted and forget that even the skilled and dedicated need time off, as well as other folks to back them up occasionally.

Time to take another inventory—of the people who lead and maintain the library's technology effort. Questions to ask in the process:

- What are the positions called?
- Are there current and accurate job descriptions for each staff member?
- How is the staff structured?
- Is the structure serving the library's needs?
- What's working well—and what's missing?
- What skill sets do the library's IT folks have? Are the important needs accounted for or do staff need to be better rounded?

INVENTORY OF STATISTICS

Many libraries collect information from users—through active and passive methods—at regular intervals. When assessing library technology, it's helpful to know what the library is collecting now—and perhaps what it should start collecting in the future.

Examples of active information collection include surveys, focus groups, and more.

Examples of passive information collection include any statistics that are automatically generated, usually through computer systems. These include information tallied by the ILS, PC management systems, bandwidth usage reports, website use statics, automated people-counting systems, and more.

USER EXPERIENCE

User experience—also known as UX—is an excellent concept to tie together all of the information collected during assessment. The nuts and bolts of assessment often result in virtual piles (and more piles) of data. Getting a sense of how people experience technology, including the pros and cons, can suggest powerful future directions and efforts.

UX is a rapidly developing field and a very worthy topic to explore further. Diving deep into UX and its many variants is beyond the scope of this book, but I suggest that all library assessment activities should at least include an investigation of how users—including public and staff—feel about their current experiences with technology.

There are many ways to discover how people feel about their technology experiences. In a future chapter, I suggest a "Dreaming and Grounding" exercise for groups to discuss and identify technology experience through the lens of successes and failures. Formal surveys are another approach, as are one-to-one or one-to-many conversations with people.

REFLECTION AND DISCUSSION—WHAT DOES THIS ALL MEAN?

Assessment activities generally result in an often intimidating collection of data. Now what? It's hardly a revelation that data can be interpreted in many different ways—and sometimes the same pools of data, viewed through different perspectives, can be cited to support widely divergent reactions. What to do?

For many library situations, I suggest reflection, discussion, and ideally a combination of both to help turn information into possibilities for action. I enjoy processing information both inside and outside—both through private thoughts, through writing and sharing, and through verbalizing with others.

Here's what works for me and my style:

- After gathering the information I need and finding/creating any evaluative resources I need (which may include comparison or ranking tools, charts and graphs, or other resources), I head to a coffee shop or other place that provides me the right space to think—away from my desk, phone, and interruptions—to read, ponder, take notes, and think. The purpose is to give myself space to draw my own conclusions about the information. Sometimes as little as thirty minutes off-site devoted to this effort gives me the time I need to turn raw data into clear vision—and leads to the formation of action steps and plans.
- Next, I commit my ideas to a written form. Sometimes a process chart, a bulleted document, a pithy vision statement—anything appropriately capturing the main ideas and clear enough to communicate to others.
- Finally, I start talking about it with others. In the process, I always discover any holes in my approach, as well many great new ideas.

Despite individual styles, it can be helpful to have a personal evaluative framework when reviewing information. Here are a few simple questions that may help guide evaluation of information:

1. What does the data indicate that the library is doing well now? What successes exist that can be built upon?

2. Does the data suggest areas of improvement?
3. Does the data suggest things that are no longer important and can be eliminated?
4. What ideas do the data present for future improvements?

Assessment takes some elbow grease. It is also an essential element of organizational planning. It's easy to become blind to the current state of any organization and to take what have long been considered "facts" for granted. Assessment activities help confirm what are thought of as facts—and sometimes challenge them to create a true and accurate picture of the state of the library.

Chapter Three

Technology Planning Part 1

The first two chapters of this book explored the broader context of technology in libraries and spent some time with practical assessment of library technology elements. Chapters 3 and 4 put those pieces into action to create a technology plan!

In chapter 3, the focus is on laying the groundwork for a successful planning process:

- defining why a technology plan is important
- determining the scope of the technology plan
- choosing good models for a technology plan
- considering a basic achievement model
- defining leadership and authority for the planning process
- handling obstacles

These initial activities can be characterized as "planning to plan"—a phrase that sometimes (and often rightfully) gets a bad rap. At its worse, pre-planning activities are used to delay or permanently postpone the important work of thinking about technology needs, creating strategies, and acting upon them. At its best, the right pre-planning moves create the strongest of foundations for technology planning and the most important aspect: the actions needed to meet goals.

It's important to note that there are many excellent approaches to planning (including entire books as well as professional disciplines such as project management professional certification and techniques adopted from software development such as Agile and Scrum). This book offers a broad overview of tips, tricks, and techniques that I've relied on in leading library technology planning. It might be helpful to think of the next two chapters as my own "greatest hits" of library technology planning methods. For readers with the desire to explore beyond the hits and venture into the "deep tracks," a rich world of discovery awaits. In the meantime, these approaches can offer a few shortcuts to creating an intentional approach to library technology.

WHY IS A TECHNOLOGY PLAN IMPORTANT?

Many librarians undoubtedly already have a firm grasp on the importance of creating operational and strategic plans to help guide institutional efforts and are familiar with clichés concerning planning (such as "Those who fail to plan, plan to fail"). But given the rapid pace of technological change, some may wonder if technology planning is really possible—or even necessary.

Not only is technology planning possible, it's vital—especially in an environment of constant change. While technology is always moving, hopefully higher-level institutional goals are more enduring and transcend the sometimes slippery environment of library technology. With an orientation toward creating solid goals and the possibility of flexible technological solutions to meet those goals, the rate of technological change can truly be an exciting asset. Over time, tech tends to get smarter, faster, more efficient, and less expensive—and hopefully provide better paths to achieve library goals.

A good technology plan is composed of certain common elements (explored in this chapter and the next) but perhaps the most important is providing the process and methods to evaluate the use of technology—or particular technological approaches—in an ongoing manner to solve problems and meet goals.

The process of technology planning has two complementary advantages:

- It results in a document to guide and help manage the library technology efforts.
- The process used to create the plan helps build skills in ongoing assessment and evaluation.

WHAT SHOULD I KNOW BEFORE STARTING?

In the next pages, the pre-planning planning process is explored step-by-step. Before starting, here are a few important considerations.

The process can be as fast or slow as needed. Ideally, a reasonable amount of time is allocated for a planning process—depending on the scope of the plan, a thorough process can take a few months or more than a year. Typically, longer planning processes include a great deal of time to gather and digest information, test hypotheses, and other activities that benefit from having a little extra time.

In many cases, technology plans are created last-minute and fast-track, often to meet deadlines such as required by grant applications or state and federal funding requirements. The need to create a quick-turnaround tech plan required for funding is a reality of library life, but even plans that are produced quickly can be effective. Ideally, even a quick-turnaround plan (which often look more like a structured "to do" list than a formal plan document) is created with some connecting thoughts to big-picture library goals. It takes work to create any plan—and it makes sense that the effort should provide impacts beyond meeting a basic requirement to secure funding.

Good planning results from the involvement of more than one person. A good technology plan requires a team to create it, research, feedback from your patrons and staff to form it, and thoughtfulness to tie it all together. Forming the right team, engaging stakeholders for input, and thoughtful activities are important steps worth time and energy.

A common approach is to "borrow" a technology plan from another library, change a few details, and call it good. After all, don't great composers steal? While this approach can make for something that looks good from a distance, it's likely to create more long-term problems than it solves. Great models exist (and I highly encourage looking at other plans for inspiration), but the best approach is to build the plan and customize an approach that will work best for each library. What's good for the goose may be good for the gander, but what's good for one library isn't necessarily good for another. A common pitfall is emulating the successful approaches of another library without first understanding why they chose a particular direction—and if library A's "why" is different than library B's, the result is often unintentional consequences. Success lies in the details, and it's up to each of us to name our own.

DETERMINING THE SCOPE OF THE TECHNOLOGY PLAN

The approach to creating a technology plan can be simple or grand, depending on the library's needs. Does your library require a very simple guide to improve day-to-day operations? Are broad, strategic directions required? The answer to these questions can help form the basis for the scope of a good technology plan.

The scope—expressed as a written description of the purpose of the technology plan—is the perfect starting point and can be thought of as the tiny seed that will grow into a magnificent plan.

It's actually the first stated goal of the plan, answering the question "What do we hope this plan accomplishes, when, and how?"

There are many factors that can influence how the scope is determined. For some it's time (it's needed now!) and for others it's impact (specific change is needed). Often it's both, and there are others as well.

Here are a few elements common to any approach to defining scope:

- Does your library need a very simple guide to improve day-to-day operations? Is the plan designed to guide broad, strategic directions? Do library needs fall somewhere in between?
- The scope should reflect other strategic plans in existence or in process. What other plans exist in the library, and how will the technology plan support and/or fit with other important efforts?
- The scope should reflect the actual implementation time for the overall plan. Since technology changes at such a rapid pace, a two- to three-year time horizon can be a fairly safe bet. Longer plans are possible, but goals beyond two to three years typically are phrased very broadly and are less specific than shorter-term goals.
- The scope should include guidelines on how many high-level goals can reasonably be accomplished in the time frame.

You may have heard the term "scope creep"—which is when the initial goals or objectives of a project organically grow or change, or new unforeseen elements are introduced to a project. Scope creep is a common challenge in any project. It's okay to change goals and objectives along the way—depending on the circumstances, it may be absolutely necessary—but the addition of changed or new goals or objectives should be a conscious decision and should be communicated to everyone affected by the change. The best defense against scope creep is simply committing your scope to written words and making sure those words are easy to refer to during the life of the project. I often write mine down on a project whiteboard and refer back periodically to see if things are still on track or if I've begun to fly a bit off the rails.

Here's an example of a statement describing the scope of a technology plan:

> The Library Technology Plan will be designed to guide broad, strategic directions for the library in full support of and alignment with the library's strategic initiatives. The plan will address a period of three years and will include three to five major goals to be achieved within the time frame of the plan.

CHOOSING A GOOD TECHNOLOGY PLAN MODEL

Despite my admonishment earlier in this chapter about one library adopting another's technology plan, I do feel that it's healthy to look to others for inspiration. A simple web search will net many examples of excellent library technology plans. While being careful to resist any temptation to directly copy the plan, there is much to be gained from finding and reading a few, taking some notes of positive and negative elements of each plan—and asking a few "why" questions. If you come up with some compelling "why" questions, I encourage you to dig more deeply and reach out to the author(s) of the plan. One of the greatest benefits of the library profession is a willingness among librarians to share information, and I've rarely come across a person who hasn't enthusiastically responded to inquiries.

As other plans are discovered and reviewed, I suggest looking for inspiration in two areas: a process model to emulate and a document model for your final plan.

Process model: these are the nuts-and-bolts steps, hopefully in sequential order, to the technology planning process. This book suggests one approach to the planning process, but there are others that may suit your needs better—either by simplifying the process or by offering more nuance.

Here's an example of a process model that I use with my clients:

Document model: what do you want your final document to look like? An easy-breezy read for your board and public, a detailed

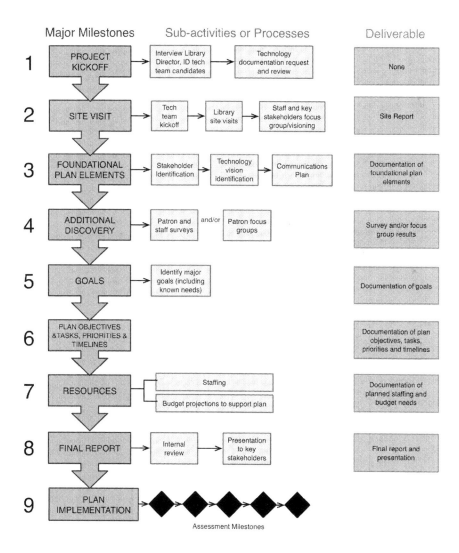

Figure 3.1. Technology Planning Process Outline

technical document to guide the nuts and bolts of the work, or something in between?

There are many document models to choose from—here's an outline of a classic example:

1. Executive Summary (includes the scope of the planning process as described earlier in this chapter)
2. Library Vision, Mission, and other elements as desired from the Library's Strategic Plan
3. Vision and Mission for the library's technology efforts
4. Overview of Broad Goals for the Technology Plan
5. Technology Plan Goals with supporting information for each goal, including:

   a. Objectives
   b. Tasks
   c. Time Frames or Deadlines

6. Evaluation Method for the Plan
7. Appendixes with the results of research and other data

TIME OUT: A LOOK AT A BASIC ACHIEVEMENT MODEL (OUR THIRD MODEL)

Along with a process model and a document model, there is a third model to consider. This model—a variation of classic project management techniques describing the basic steps to achievement—could make the difference between an efficient, directed process and one that wanders and stalls until it dies on the vine.

This process is deceptively simple, and at the beginning of a planning effort, it may seem unnecessary. But as the planning process continues, things will grow more complex. Those tasked with the planning process will be gathering and synthesizing lots of new information from a variety of sources. More people and personal-

Figure 3.2. Achieve Plan

ities with different viewpoints and styles will join the mix. What seems simple at first can quickly become complex and confusing. Using this model can help keep the process pure, and you can devote your personal and shared brain power to other tasks. And this model scales up and down—you can use it to guide the grandest and most complex project all the way down to the simplest tasks. As another plus—it's a "meta" opportunity to run through a mini-version of a plan to create the technology plan!

Here are how the steps break out.

Identify High-Level Goals

It's important to do a good job of identifying the high-level goals of any project or the entire process is at risk. These are the outcomes you desire, and they should be simple and clear enough to be written down. Every decision made along the way—from small to big—should be tested against these. If later in the process it seems that the original goals are eroding (remember "scope creep"?), it's time to revisit the goals and either confirm and strengthen your original direction or formally change your high-level goals to reflect your current situation. Either response is perfectly fine, but it should always be a deliberate decision that is understood among participants in the planning process.

Design Tasks and Options

Tasks do not drive high-level objectives. For instance, things shouldn't be done simply because they are easy or avoided just because they are difficult. The tasks to complete the planning process, whatever they are, should support the achievement of the high-level goals. To be successful, we need to commit to the resources needed to accomplish the tasks. If you find that the difficulty of performing the tasks are cooling the enthusiasm for the goals of the planning process, it's time to reassess those high-level goals and either recommit or change them.

Deal with Obstacles

Obstacles do not drive high-level goals. Perhaps the most controversial part of the achievement model, I believe, is that obstacles are often given more power than they warrant when trying to identify goals. Sometimes it's tempting to grab that low-hanging fruit, but somehow I know the best tasting is way atop the tree . . .

One way to approach facing obstacles without altering your high-level goals or objectives is to use "and" statements. For instance, let's assume a library has a deep desire to convert its collection to use Radio Frequency Identification (RFID) but is fearful of the costs required. Exploring a thoughtful question like "What options can we discover to implement RFID *and* at an affordable budget?" This approach of keeping the goal intact can rob obstacles of any disproportionate power and can help uncover new solutions and approaches.

Achieve Plan! 'Nuff said.

LEADERSHIP AS RELATED TO THE PLANNING PROCESS

To set the stage for a successful planning process, here is a handful of simple housekeeping tips before launching the planning process.

Organizational support: support for the planning process from on high is crucial. Who is your higher power? This is not a question of religion (although faith is often involved) but of making sure your actual or figurative "boss"—a person, committee, or anyone else in your leadership chain—understands the goals of the planning process, knows how you plan to proceed with the process, and is in total support of it. They may even participate in molding the scope of the planning process, which is a sure path to buy-in and support.

Identify team leader and structure: every team needs both a leader and a structure. The leader can have any number of styles (from laissez-faire to authoritarian and anywhere in between or beyond)—but no matter the style, the leader is the person responsible to set the tone, inspire the team, and ensure all tasks are completed. The team leader will undoubtedly structure the team in a way that complements their preferred approach. Under good leadership, any team structure can be successful, but it's important that someone is tasked with the responsibility of ensuring the planning process is launched, followed through with, and completed. In some cases, "team leadership" (perhaps two or more individuals sharing leadership duties) is possible—and requires individuals with high levels of personal accountability, a strong sense of responsibility, and the highest levels of trust between the team co-leaders.

For the next steps in the planning process described in this book, I will assume there is one team leader.

AUTHORITY AND OBSTACLE MANAGEMENT

Define leadership authority: often, teams are composed of folks from different parts of the organization, including peers and people in higher positions of authority. In many cases, the technology planning process will not be led by the library director but by someone else lower in the authority chain. In the heat of the process, the team leader may need to assign work to and/or hold accountable someone over whom they normally have no authority.

It's wise to think through how to successfully manage potential conflicts if they arise.

Obstacle management: another key element to determine up front is the process to manage obstacles. I believe the majority of obstacles (both real and potential) in any effort are foreseeable when we can take the time to think through each step in the process and do some scenario planning—and imagine what options we have if we hit snags along the way.

- Conflicts happen—with time schedules, between personalities on your team, and in ever-growing and often surprising areas. Determining in advance the methods to help resolve potential conflicts helps ensure momentum during tough times.
- Tough decisions are part of the process. To define most of the elements of your plan, the team leader and the team will be required to make choices from an almost infinite number of possibilities. Determining in advance the process to tackle difficult decisions also assists forward motion for the planning process.

Determining how to handle these up front will save you time and stress later. When any of these obstacles appear, you will be ready to address them. It's a beautiful part of the planning process!

Chapter Four

Technology Planning Part 2

In this chapter, we take on the actual planning process (which some may consider to be the "real work" of planning). For those of us who like to dive right into action, a pre-planning process as described in chapter 3 can seem cumbersome. Planning does take time—and even planning how to go about a planning process can be a significant chunk of the "real work." I've found that doing the right amount of up-front work is a good investment of time and effort that makes the next steps in the process go smoothly and offers the best chance of achieving the goals and objectives of the planning process. In my personal experiences, every time I've had a good pre-planning process, I've had excellent plan execution. When I've given pre-planning short shrift, I generally had to spend a maddening amount of time reacting to problems that kept pushing my goals and objectives farther and farther away from completion.

This chapter covers the following actions in creating a technology plan:

- forming a planning team
- running good meetings
- promoting creativity and realism through group activities
- researching and compiling the results

- writing the plan
- providing for change
- soliciting reviews and approvals

FORMING A PLANNING TEAM

A good team is an excellent asset to the technology planning process. The team will not just help do the work but ensure that the work is done well. The key then is to pick team members who bring positive and complementary skills to the table. Teams can be as tiny as two or as large as a dozen, but don't try to tackle a technology plan without a team.

A team should be reflective of the staff makeup of the institution, including those with intimate knowledge of the people whom you serve. If the library is composed of a system of branches, it's important to have geographic representation—including neighborhoods or regions of the library system. Look for a mix of staff from all levels in the library hierarchy, including folks at the bottom of it. It's not a stretch to consider that managers may not have the time to keep up with technology trends, while shelvers may already be living a full-on native digital lifestyle and have invaluable insights to share. Needless to say, the IT manager or staff (if the library has either) should be represented on the team—depending on the library, the IT department may even lead the planning team.

Ideally, team members should have individual skills and orientations that complement each other: big-picture thinkers and detail-oriented logisticians; specialists and generalists; early adopters and technophobes; cynics and optimists; pontificators and folks who know the work isn't done until they've rolled up their sleeves and made it happen; and other opposites who should be attracted to create a complementary blend of skills and sensitivities.

Putting together a good team is an art form in itself, and it's true that the more diverse the team, the more of a chore it can be to manage. But harnessing a team with diverse and complementary skills—pointed in the right direction—can produce priceless results.

RUNNING GOOD MEETINGS AND OTHER GATHERINGS

After assembling a team, the natural next step is to gather people together—usually in the form of a meeting. Here are a few methods that I've found to be effective in moving from ideas to action. A key aspect of inspiring any team member—and the team as a whole—to give their very best is to show them how much you respect members' time by not wasting it. A key action is running good meetings.

Have an Agenda

Many of us have experienced the unpleasantness of meetings that meandered on a pointless path and resulted in no clear outcomes. I would guess that most of us have experienced that particular pain more than once. Chances are those meetings didn't have an agenda (or if they did, the agenda was not observed). But an agenda itself won't prevent bad craziness—and all agendas are not created equal.

There are many good models for agendas, but they don't need to be complicated. Essentially a good agenda should include:

- the amount of time scheduled for the meeting (and don't go longer without the full consent of the group)
- the topics to be covered
- decisions that need to be made
- a place to record outcomes and decisions from discussions
- a place to record follow-up actions and who is responsible for those actions
- supporting information, data, and other resources

Simple, right?

Define Expectations, Roles, and Schedules

As well as an agenda that clearly defines the content and expectations of the meeting, each team member should have a clear idea of
the big picture and their part in it. The team leader should use the
first meeting to voice expectations of the team, any particular roles
expected of individuals (and it's perfectly fine to seek volunteers),
and the schedule for the project. In many cases, these items are
determined in a collaborative fashion.

Foster Team Culture from the Beginning

The first meeting is the most important—it will set the tone for all
others to follow. Clichés aside about "first impressions," I believe
that during the first meeting, the leader and members alike begin
forming opinions about each other's competence, skills, integrity,
and even likability within the context of the planning effort. In
many ways, these first impressions dictate the flow of the planning
process. I hope the pressure of conducting a great launch meeting
both inspires and worries team leaders a little—a lot is at stake, and
a planning process is a great deal of work that deserves an excellent
and deliberate start.

The first meeting offers others an excellent opportunity to build
team culture, including shared team values. Need a shortcut to cul-
tivating team culture? I suggest sparking a conversation that explores an element of the library's existing statement of vision or
values and asking how that current element applies to the library's
technology efforts—and perhaps how things could be improved.
Another juicy topic might be discussing what "user-centered" technology means in a library environment.

One other note on running a good meeting—all teams have
norms or other "rules" whether they are formally expressed or not,
and it usually falls to the leader to enforce the rules. Instead of

unspoken rules, I suggest discussing and writing them down. The list needn't be long or complicated. It might look something like this:

- Everyone has the right to participate.
- We will encourage each other.
- We will share our thoughts.
- We will actively listen and show respect for each other.
- Criticism should always be constructive.
- Debate is encouraged—and tough subjects will be voted on, decided by consensus, decided by the team leader, or other method.

Dreaming and Grounding

Remember how radio personality Casey Kasem used to sign off his broadcasts? "Keep your feet on the ground and keep reaching for the stars." (Kasem was also the voice of Shaggy on the old Scooby Doo cartoons and was the featured voice in a controversial audio performance piece entitled "The Letter U and the Numeral 2," which is an interesting story of intellectual property rights in the age of new media. But I digress.)

It's not only possible to lead a group through an exercise to simultaneously dream big and establish solid footing on Terra Firma, but it's also a great way to illustrate the daily dynamic of technology. Every day I walk into work with a list of technology-related tasks to accomplish. Likewise, every day multiple aspects of technology undergo both minor and major changes, with many of the changes directly related to my tasks. Bridging the reality and the dream is part of the job. Revealing this to my teams, especially those new to technology projects, helps capture the zeitgeist and creates the right mindset for the work to come.

Properly done, this exercise can accomplish many things in one fell swoop, including identifying vision, taking an institutional temperature check, shaking out new ideas, and other things.

One method is asking the group three deceptively simple questions and capturing the discussion on a whiteboard that has been divided like this:

What is our current experience with technology in the library? Technology is...	What could we improve? We want to implement technology that...	What is our wish for the future? We want technology that...

Figure 4.1.   Three Whiteboard Questions

The questions above needn't be answered in any particular order, and the answers to these open-ended queries can be as broad or specific as the participants like and still be useful to the process. I've found that once the ball is rolling, a deep and shared understanding can be discovered in a very short time.

For an example of one result from such a discussion, see figure 4.2. In this case, the discussion brought all team members together to identify where the library came from, where it is now, and where it wants to go technologically.

There are lots of excellent alternatives, including the classic SWOT discussion—an examination of Strengths, Weaknesses, Opportunities, and Threats. For more information on that process, see http://en.wikipedia.org/wiki/SWOT_analysis.

DELIVERABLES FROM THE FIRST TEAM MEETINGS

As team leader, you can determine any mix of deliverables that suit your needs, and depending on the time available, it may take several meetings to produce the deliverables that will become elements of the technology plan.

Based on the classic technology plan outline discussed in the previous chapter, here is a list of items to get you started.

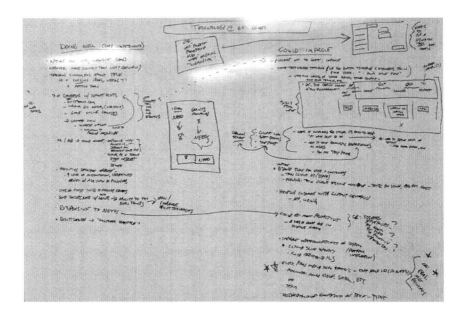

Figure 4.2. Whiteboard Example

Identify Institutional Vision and Mission

The technology planning team, of course, will not create these statements, but should discuss and carry them through to ensure that the technology plan is aligned with the greater goals of the organization. If you find that the library has not named its vision and mission, it might be time to stop technology planning and turn the attention to overall institutional planning!

Identify Vision and Mission for the Library's Technology Efforts

What is the role of technology in a particular library? This could come from your technology planning committee—perhaps as a result of your dreaming and grounding exercise. Ideas and concepts could also come from patrons, the governing body, library leadership, or staff. Wherever it comes from, it should resonate with those groups, and the technology planning committee is in the perfect position to form statements that work and guide.

Identify Primary Stakeholders and Possible Engagement Opportunities

The purpose of identifying technology plan stakeholders is to ensure awareness of those affected by the technology efforts of the library and consider each when determining technology plan elements. In some cases, the technology planning team may engage the groups that have been identified through interviews, surveys, or focus groups. In other cases, some stakeholders will simply be placed in "front of mind" as the team considers technology plan elements. Stakeholders can be defined as broadly or as specifically as is useful for the planning process.

In cases when the planning team includes the library director and staff members (including a member from the IT department), the technology planning team can be representative of the major stakeholder groups: patrons (via staff perspectives), library management and staff (directly), and IT support (directly).

Primary Stakeholders and Engagement

Here's an example of how one technology planning team identified the following *primary stakeholders* and engaged them in various ways, including *interviews, focus groups*, and *surveys*:

Table 4.1.

Stakeholder	Engagement Method
library director	interviews and focus groups
library staff	focus groups and technology planning team
library patrons—users of in-house technology	electronic survey
library patrons—users of web technology	electronic survey
library patrons—WiFi users	electronic survey

Create a Chart of the Process

Although the actual steps will be based on your specific model, there are some tasks common to most planning processes:

- planning team meetings
- research (including data harvesting, surveys, focus groups, and other sources and/or activities)
- selection of plan goals
- writing
- plan reviews and approvals
- communications (along the way and at the end of the process)

Using the sample process from chapter 3, the version in figure 4.3 has a draft timeline in a new column to the right.

Depending on the style of the team leader, the initial meeting may start with a broad, simple outline of tasks involved or a firm schedule. The team leader may also choose to task the team or a portion of the team with drafting a schedule for the planning process.

Identify Communications Plan

With your timeline in hand to help guide your team, you might feel ready to roll. Pause for a moment and determine how you will keep everyone else who needs to know—or who are simply interested—up to date as the planning process progresses.

Your draft timeline can do double duty as a communications tool, but you can also use e-mail, blog posts, Facebook or Twitter updates, a tool such as #slack or Basecamp, the library's intranet (if one exists), or whatever methods you use to regularly connect yourself to others.

Major Milestones   Sub-activities or Processes   Deliverable

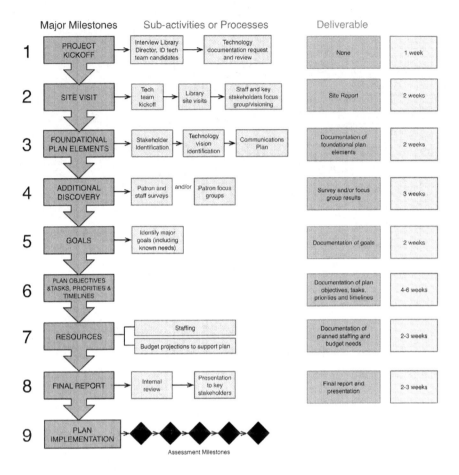

Figure 4.3.   Technology Planning Process Outline 2

Assign Responsibilities

As part of the meeting process, it's important to establish shared responsibilities for tasks. Trust me, though—don't let anyone leave the room without taking some level of responsibility for the completion of tasks. Remember—this is a process that benefits from the contributory efforts of a team. You will need a team not just for the planning, but also for ensuring that tasks actually get completed! A good team helps hold each other accountable—and helps each other achieve the shared objectives.

If you follow our outline, you will want to make sure you have people from your committee assigned to these important next steps:

• compilation
• writing
• review

What do your patrons need from technology? What do they want from technology? What would you like to do with technology? Some simple research can help you find the answer to those questions.

Think back to when we talked about whom you serve, what you have (in terms of technology—your technology inventory), and what you offer. Now it's time to build on those pieces and expand them to help create your technology plan.

Most libraries have two primary publics using technology: patrons and staff. And depending on your level of sophistication, you might even further subdivide those groups into the specific technologies they use (for instance, you might want to consider users of your website as a separate group).

Let's assume the simplest situation for now—two groups of users: patrons and staff. As part of planning, you might consider asking these users a couple of questions:

• How well does the library's technology serve your current needs?
• Are you able to find what you want on our website?
• What can we do to serve you better?
• What new technology support might serve you in the future?
• What else would you like to know?

There are many venues to consider when asking these questions. For instance, for users of the library website, an electronic survey is an appropriate venue. For patrons and staff using your physical computing resources, you can use the convenience of electronic surveys or convene some focus groups, forums, or brown-bag lunches.

Whatever method you choose should give you confidence that you've heard and understood the input, and the people you've asked should also feel heard and understood. Later, when the plan is in play, that will lend credibility to both your planning process and the plan itself.

Compilation

Gathering the data is half of the job—the other halves (as Yogi Berra might say) are compiling it, reviewing it, and deciding what influence it will have for your technology plan. If you used a survey site (like Google Forms or SurveyMonkey), you had the option to learn how to construct a survey that presented you with clear, actionable information. If you held focus groups, you had the opportunity to see what needs or issues most of the group had in common. Both methods build compilation right into the process!

Once your surveys or focus groups are complete, and the data is compiled in an easy-to-read and hopefully easy-to-understand format, it's time to pull the planning team together to review. Depending on how much time you have, you might want to assign members of the teams to draw and suggest conclusions from the data, or you might want to even do that yourself. The team should discuss and agree on the major conclusions.

You will have one more step to perform before writing—it's time to look back to the beginning of the planning process and review your scope. What was the result of the "dreaming and grounding" exercise? How much time is given for the plan to be complete? How many major objectives are reasonable to accomplish in that time? It's time to match the vision and conclusions with some high-level goals.

After goals are identified, the next step is generally to identify objectives, the tasks to support those objectives, and some reasonable deadlines for each task. Finally, consider how you will measure progress on the plan—and how often you would like to provide a progress report.

Writing: From Buckets to Goals—and Ultimately a Plan

The technology plan has been quite a process—and now it all comes down to the final document capturing, well, everything—and naming your technological targets for the future.

Now is the time to bring out a "document model" to refresh memories on how to apply the preferred format for the final technology plan. Many technology plans could fit into the following framework:

- a little about the library (vision/mission)
- a little about the library's current technology effort (including an inventory of current technology resources)
- a little about the library's philosophy toward technology
- separate sections for each high-level goal, supporting objectives, supporting tasks, deadlines, and how progress will be measured
- appendixes for any raw data (from surveys or focus groups) that should be shared

The technology plan elements are typically determined in this order:

1. plan vision
2. plan buckets
3. plan goals
4. plan objectives
5. plan tasks
6. plan priorities
7. plan timeline

8. plan resources

Tip: if you're not used to it, writing can be tough. Be sure to have your best writers take the lead, and create a way for someone else (a co-writer or an "editor") to help with the back-and-forth that is part of any good writing process. Write, review, edit, and repeat until done!

The structure of Goals > Objectives > Tasks and Timelines is deceptively simple; actually writing a plan in this format can sometimes be difficult. Here's one approach to try if you're stuck when trying to form all the elements to date into the format of a technology plan.

Buckets

The purpose of the "buckets" for the technology plan is to create the basis for the major plan *goals*. "Buckets" are a figurative place where the team groups discovery and research information (from various sources) to create areas of possible synergy when designing solutions. This information is generally in a mix of formats—including big ideas, specific technological approaches, gripes, aspirations, good ideas and also some bad ones. Creating buckets is a way to sort through all of this information and organize it into themes. The buckets exercise is generally an iterative team activity and is usually as simple as asking "What trends do we see?" followed by "What 'buckets' might these trends fall into?"

Once a few good buckets are identified, the next step is placing the discovery elements within the bucket categories. There are many methods to do this—from sticky notes on a whiteboard to spreadsheets. The idea is to stay big picture to ensure the major categories captured in the buckets are covering what you need.

Typically, the technology planning team strives to have a small number of major plan goals, with three to five being optimal. The goals are supported by objectives and plan tasks, followed by identification of resources (including time—expressed as a timeline—staffing, and budget).

Review and Adjustment

Throughout the process, each major plan component will be revisited as needed until the plan is complete. Review of resources often requires adjustments to the plan elements prior to the plan being finalized, but should not be the initial consideration in the planning process to avoid missing any possibilities. Over time, new resources may emerge (including funding, grants, partnerships, and other sources), so it's important that the first draft of the plan include an unencumbered collection of what the team believes are crucial elements of the technology plan.

THINGS CHANGE—HOW TO ALLOW FOR IT IN A TECHNOLOGY PLAN

This advice is short but hopefully sweet: allow for change in your plan by giving yourself the option to decide to not complete something on it in the future.

There are a lot of good reasons why you may not be able to complete something on your technology plan. What seems hot today can quickly cool tomorrow. Variations in budgets can change the institutional priorities dramatically. Leadership positions can change. Institutionally, you may simply lose interest. It's fair game to reflect that reality in your plan.

Here's some text I used in the last technology plan I created. Feel free to use it!

> Resources to provide for patron and staff needs—in terms of both dollars and staff hours—are finite, and this plan expresses the technology priorities for the next two years. As the new areas detailed in this plan are explored and accomplished, IT staff will consistently evaluate existing efforts and services. It's

likely that when prioritizing efforts, the IT department (with appropriate transition planning) will "stop doing" things that no longer support the library's top priorities.

REVIEWS AND APPROVALS

The final steps in your technology plan usually include a series of reviews, starting with your committee. Once your committee likes the document, it's time for it to make the rounds before it becomes official.

Typically, review groups will include the library management team, the director, the public, and any advisory or governing board your library might have. Before launching the review cycle, decide what you're asking for—simple acknowledgment or the opportunity to mold the plan further? Since different approaches can drastically impact the amount of time it would take to finalize the plan, choose wisely and appropriately for your situation.

Chapter Five

Technology Implementation

A freshly minted technology plan is just sitting there, waiting to guide library efforts and delight patrons and staff with a deliberate approach to meeting needs and forging new directions. Now that a process has been completed to plan the work, it's time to work the plan! This chapter considers strategies designed to turn the words and ideas of the plan into action—and avoid pitfalls that can stand in the way.

Key concepts in technology implementation include:

- making the plan a priority
- starting efforts before the plan is completed
- creating a planning calendar
- monitoring and sharing progress
- forming implementation teams
- managing implementation plans
- bringing stakeholders together
- managing the technology budget
- what about new things? (or the lure of the bright, shiny object)
- the tyranny of the urgent

MAKING THE PLAN A PRIORITY

Typically, there are two things that can happen when a technology planning process is wrapped up—moving full speed ahead on the plan or "filing" the plan to perhaps refer to at a future date. Here's how the scenarios often play out:

1. Full speed ahead: in this scenario, it is likely that some elements of the plan have been implemented—or at least started—before the ink was dry on the final version of the plan. Deadlines and other date targets are posted to calendars. Teams are formed when needed. Vendors are contacted and bids are placed. Stakeholders are brought together (often as specified in the plan) to contribute to the process. Efforts are monitored and progress is shared (again, often as specified in the plan). Things are tried: successes are built upon, and failures provide an opportunity to try new approaches in pursuit of the goals and objectives. Successes are celebrated!

2. Filing the plan for possible future reference: in this scenario, the plan (if printed) excels at collecting dust. If it's printed, it's probably under a stack of other papers. Perhaps it's reviewed annually (during annual report time), which tends to be a depressing experience since the plan was not woven into the fabric of the library's efforts. Upon review, readers see lost opportunities. The whole idea of a planning process— and the work entailed—becomes suspect.

It's not a stretch to guess that scenario number 1 is the only one I find acceptable. Sadly, I've seen scenario number 2 play out too often. During the planning process, it's likely that the "do-ers" in the library became frustrated because they just wanted to start working on things (and didn't have a lot of patience for all the process involved). Indeed, a planning process is a mighty effort, but the real work begins when the plan is done and it's time for the rubber to hit the road.

STARTING EFFORTS BEFORE THE PLAN IS COMPLETED

Some ideas are so good—or so time sensitive—that there is a strong temptation to start them before the planning process is wrapped up. While there is some risk in implementing ideas before the plan is completed, it's not necessarily a bad thing.

Depending on the size of the library, sometimes "official" plan approvals can take almost as long as the planning process itself. In the meantime, though, it's likely that some important (and fundamental) tasks can be performed—and as with all matters of technology, time is ticking. Whether and how to start efforts before the planning process is completed is one of those things that falls to a leadership decision—and might play out differently if the leader is the library director, technology staff, or others involved.

Although each situation is different, I'll share two examples where getting a head start was essential to progress for the library.

"We need a new leader." I've been involved in several situations when, in the process of planning, the team determined that a key part of the library's needs lay in restructuring the technology leadership. In several cases, that meant hiring a whole new sort of leader—in most cases transitioning from an "IT-centric" manager to a "technology innovation" leadership position that would oversee the IT department but also provide strategic and direct connection to the library's public service efforts. With such a radical change, it made sense to slow the planning process for a bit to hire the new leader and invite them into the planning process. After all, we wanted the new technology leader to "own" and successfully implement the technology plan, and what better way to ensure that than inviting them to have a strong role in creating the plan?

"A basic step is going to take a lot of time. We need to start now!" In a planning process for a longtime library technology consortium (providing ILS, network, and other services), we discovered that no one—including the consortium management and staff, the "owners" of the consortium, and most importantly the client libraries—had a shared understanding of current services, levels of services, and the role of the consortium and client libraries around those services. In this case, instead of just creating a goal to fix that issue as part of the plan to implement later, we created a document describing the current state of services and consortium leaders began communicating with members immediately to gather feedback and refine.

There are risks in starting efforts early, including not having all the needed information or being unaware of crucial dependencies. Early implementers should also have excellent project management skills (especially in being able to alter course on the fly) and be ready for surprises. When at all possible, it's best to just button up the planning process as quickly as possible and move forward, but some things just shouldn't wait.

CREATING A PLANNING CALENDAR

During the planning process, a "timeline" is sometimes created, showing how the activities of the plan may occur over time. When implementing, it's time to transfer that timeline to a real calendar!

There are many tools available to help manage projects—and indeed the portfolio of projects created by a good technology plan. Specific project management approaches and disciplines are not covered in this book—there are many excellent ways to manage projects, the success of which relies on how the method suits the people or the teams involved.

One thing common to all project management methods is time and the simple act of posting project time frames and deadlines to a calendar, especially a shared one.

We live in a time of ubiquitous collaboration tools—from Google's slate of calendar- and document-sharing tools, to collaboration platforms from #slack, Basecamp, Microsoft, and many others. I love (and use) many online tools—the key is using tools that work best for the organization. As a consultant, that means I don't use just one platform but many. My measure is determining what works best for each library or library system. If people don't like the platform or method, they won't participate, and it's "game over" in terms of successful project management.

Since the response to electronic tools is highly variable, and although I hope anyone implementing a technology plan is also using electronic calendaring as a tool (and sharing it with others), I will suggest a tried-and-true analog approach: a poster-sized paper (or dry-erase) planning calendar. Some key elements include:

- The entire date range of the plan should always be visible. Depending on the length of the plan, this could take up a lot of wall space so the format should be chosen accordingly.
- Since change is a constant, the tool should be flexible to use. If using a paper calendar, I suggest posting Goals, Objectives, and Actions using sticky notes (which can be moved as needed). Dry-erase boards are another flexible approach.
- Decide the purpose of the calendar. When I just need to keep myself on track, I've posted it in my office. When I want others to see it too, I've posted it in a more accessible place.

The planning calendar is an important implementation step—not only can one see how activities are planned to occur over time, but in the process of posting these in a linear format, most implementers also begin thinking through and identifying the smaller steps involved in an effort—including pre-work, possibilities for com-

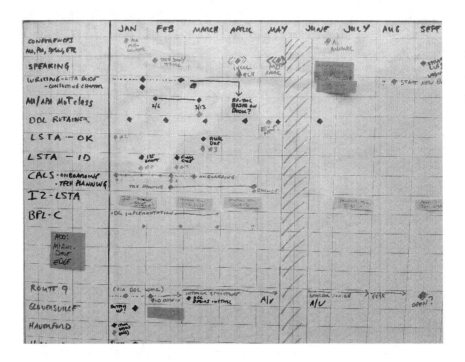

Figure 5.1. Planning Calendar Example. *Even a simple white-board—such as the author's planning calendar from 2016—can be a helpful organizational tool.*

bining actions, and possible schedule conflicts. For fun, many implementers think of the calendar as a "game board" and the actions are game pieces that all fit together to compete a beautiful plan! Thinking through this is also a trigger for important work—such as contacting vendors when needed (big or expensive efforts may require special purchasing procedures such as an RFP process), putting together implementation teams, and more.

MONITORING AND SHARING PROGRESS

A key item for a planning calendar should be lifted directly from the technology plan: the designated milestones to track, record, and share progress on the plan. Depending on the library, this can be a very informal process (a verbal chat—at planned intervals—between the implementer and his or her supervisor) or part of official proceedings such as board or trustee meetings. For some (such as some IT shops in libraries), it's even a regular part of staff meetings!

Many people are afraid of "blowing deadlines," which makes many reticent to monitor and share process. I understand that fear, but I want to encourage everyone to embrace the monitoring/sharing process as a powerful approach to successfully completing the projects on the technology plan. I think what hinders many is not knowing how to adjust when things don't go as envisioned. Figure 5.2 shows a reporting template to use that can keep everyone posted and the plan moving forward.

Over the time period of the plan, the library will report progress to the library board every six months. Using the planning time frame as a basis, the library will provide a simple report using one of these options.

FORMING IMPLEMENTATION TEAMS

In libraries with enough staff, taking a "team" approach to implementation is a powerful force. Since libraries are service-oriented, people-centered organizations, a good technology implementation team can be built from staff of all stripes. In fact, in the case of a technology project affecting a particular group or department in the library, it's essential to include that group or department in rolling out the tech. Hopefully, they were already included during the planning process when needs were identified and goals and actions were formed.

Teams often get a bad rap, though, due to some common pitfalls in the teaming process. Here are a few examples of good and bad teams:

Status	Example
Scheduled Objective and/or Task is complete	"This objective and/or task was completed within/before the scheduled time. Here is the outcome...."
Scheduled Objective and/or Task is partially complete	"This objective and/or task was not completed within the scheduled time. These factors {...} were unforeseen and this is the new schedule timeline."
Scheduled Task and/or Objective has been eliminated (Why?)	"This objective and/or task was not completed and was eliminated from the plan for the following reasons."
Scheduled Task and/or Objective has been deferred (Why? and When?)	"This objective and/or task has been deferred for the following reasons, once these issues are resolved this objective and/or task will be revisited."
A new Task and/or Objective has been identified (Please list using the same format as other technology plan tasks or objectives.)	When writing a new task and/or objective there should be a way to measure how that objective/ task was achieved or not achieved and why the new task and/or objective was needed/ created. • For example, the task/objective must be specific and concrete. Instead of saying " there must be an increase of server uptime", say instead " server uptime must meet a minimum of 90% within a 6 month time period". • List needs in completion or needs order • Every task and/or objective needs to be given a date to work towards either completion or review. When no dates are assigned then nothing is a priority

Figure 5.2.   Reporting Template

One definition of a good team: a group of individuals with complementary skills united by clear purpose and guided by strong leadership—and those who lead the team should approach that role as a servant—and in service—to the team. Sometimes even great teams fail to meet their objectives, but they always brush off any difficulties and keep trying until tasks are completed because great teams are built for performance and the abilities of the team as a whole outstrip any of the individual skill sets. Simply put, a good team loves to meet challenges and solve problems—and solve them together.

A bad team...	A good team...
...offers a venue to avoid responsibility and accountability.	...offers a venue to ensure responsibility and accountability.
...is an amorphous entity with an ill-defined purpose, scope and expectations.	...has a clear purpose, including a well-defined scope and expectations.
...is something to blame when the work does not go as expected	...is something to rely on to persevere when the work does not go as expected.

Figure 5.3. Reporting Template Option 1

I'm not sure my definition is listed in Webster's or Wikipedia, but it describes the best teams I've been privileged to be a part of. I also realize it describes an ideal that may or may not be easily attainable (the leadership part is tricky and a worthy topic for further study outside of this book). Nevertheless, in an age of tight budgets and high expectations, focusing on building strong, healthy teams is the only real hedge in a rapidly changing world and is an investment that pays dividends far beyond the time and money invested.

MANAGING IMPLEMENTATION TEAMS

An implementation team is different from the team formed for the technology planning process. If the human resources are available, this team is probably made mostly from IT professionals who are devoted to the IT needs of the library. In some cases, though, this team could be formed from what are called "accidental" technologists—in other words, bright, eager staff with an interest and aptitude for technology but little or no formal training.

Forming an ideal implementation team is one of the riskiest ventures a person can undertake because a good team is made up of people with complementary skill sets. A less diplomatic way to put it is that the strongest teams are made from people who might be polar opposites—individuals with very different skill sets and perhaps on the surface nothing in common. When these opposites are properly paired to accomplish the work at hand, it creates a powerful positive force. When not properly paired, their differences can equally tear things apart.

This is where leadership comes in. If one peers beyond the surface, even people with vastly different personalities, styles, skills, and strengths can have common core beliefs and characters, sharing values—moral, quality of work, respect, and more. The job of a good leader is to find the people with both complementary skills and similar core values and fit them together like a beautiful jigsaw puzzle.

If common core beliefs and characteristics are not evident in team members, headway can still be made in this area. As part of the objective-setting process, a team leader can also suggest/test beliefs and values with the aim of getting support from the team members.

For instance, there have been times when managing a technology project that I've had a tight timeline and didn't have the time to thoroughly pilot or test before implementing a solution. In one case, I discussed with my team the proactive/reactive concept prevalent among technologists (discussed earlier in the book) and then asked the question "Given the short time frame, does a reactive posture make sense in this situation? Can we agree to proceed without further study and testing and build time in later to react to issues?" I can offer no guarantees on the outcome of such a discussion, but in most of the cases I've been involved in, working through it brings forward very healthy dialogue, authentic buy-in from the team, and ultimately wise choices.

This subject is a topic of further study outside of this book but is an element to consider as you approach building your teams.

BRINGING STAKEHOLDERS TOGETHER

Regardless of background or expertise, many have experienced a particularly dreadful experience: instead of being delighted by the joy of successful implementation of a new technological approach, they feel more like technology has been "done to them." In these cases, not only is the adoption of the particular technology clunky, but it leaves a lingering bad taste about technology in general.

One way to avoid this horrible situation is to do a little advance work: think through who is affected by a technological change and ensure that they are brought into the process in some appropriate manner. For some, that means including them in any technology planning process—but for others it could be as simple as engaging them to help plan an implementation that will be affecting them.

There are as many scenarios as there are technologies, but here's a general framework that can work in many situations.

1. Take an inventory of stakeholders. Who is directly affected by this change? Who might be indirectly affected? Who has been forgotten (dig deep)?
2. How deeply is each stakeholder group affected? Will the implementation interrupt their daily work? Will the new technology change how they perform their work?
3. Communication is key, and methods vary for each stakeholder group. In most cases, stakeholders who are directly affected should be brought into the process as early as possible to help design the change, identify possible pitfalls, and help coordinate schedules. It seems like everyone still uses e-mail for communications, but it's important to remember that most forms of communications are "one way at a time" and can contribute to communications failures. By setting a goal of

ensuring that key people are informed, the possibilities are endless and should include the communications methods that work best for the stakeholders. For some, that means modern communications methods (including threaded discussion lists and text messaging), and for others, that may mean video chats, telephone calls, or in-person opportunities including one-on-one and meetings.

4. Engagement methods also vary. In some of the best cases, the planned changes were requested by stakeholders, and it can be highly successful to bring them in early to help plan the process, identify success factors, spot trouble areas, assist with different pieces of the effort, and evangelize the changes to other staff afterward.

MANAGING THE TECHNOLOGY BUDGET

I've already posited that we don't save money with technology but instead spend it with the result of realizing institutional efficiencies. With that outlook, some might expect me to pontificate about loosening budget constraints, spending freely, or essentially opening up the ol' wallet and letting funds flow freely. Not a chance.

Technology spending can be a model of efficiency or a deep, dark, bottomless hole that consumes all the cash thrown at it with nary a tangible result. Budgets need to be created and carefully monitored to ensure our libraries are on the efficient side and far away from that black hole of spending.

Mastering tech budgets is outside of the scope of this book, but here are few simple concepts to apply when budgeting for technology.

Ongoing monies are expenses that are expected to be spent on a regular basis and include things like desktop computer replacement, annual maintenance and service contracts, and others. Care should be taken to actively evaluate ongoing monies in an ongoing fashion and to especially be aware of areas that can be trimmed annually because they are no longer needed (like typewriter repair) and areas that should be shored up (like network infrastructure replacement).

New projects are generally best considered investments—money spent up front with the intent of longer-term gain. Depending on scope and scale, projects can range from shoestring affairs to significant cash outlays. To determine whether budgets are reasonable, the project plan should include a "Return on Investment" or ROI component—measuring things like higher efficiencies, creating more and better resources and services for the same dollars, and (yes) even saving money in some cases.

New technologies should be enthusiastically explored and understood but, from a budgetary angle, cautiously deployed. If an expensive new approach perfectly matches institutional and technology priorities, it's probably a good investment. Being on the bleeding edges costs the most in money and risk with the potential of the greatest rewards, leading edge less so on all three fronts, and behind the curve even less! Identifying where the library and the technology staff is on the "edge" continuum can help guide the approach to adopting new technologies.

Free technologies should also be enthusiastically explored and understood, but the concept of "no such thing as a free lunch" comes into play here. It's important to peek under the hood to understand how the provider or vendor is directly or indirectly compensated for their product or service. What is being traded, in terms of data or access, for the service? Sometimes it's a good trade; other times it's not—but all cases require a special look. The same filter can be applied to free open-source technologies. I love open source, but I also know that it requires a commitment of time, which equates to dollars. It's often worth it (on many levels, including paying it forward), but it's also not exactly free.

WHAT ABOUT NEW THINGS? OR THE LURE OF THE BRIGHT, SHINY OBJECT

As technology plans are implemented, it seems that almost immediately new technologies, new ideas, and new processes spring up—things that were not considered earlier in the planning process. It's completely natural to consider how to incorporate new ideas and approaches.

Making decisions whether and how to incorporate new ideas can be a snap. With solid goals defined—those high-level statements defining the achievement targets in the technology plan—new opportunities can emerge and become a wonderful smorgasbord of options. Does the exciting new technology recently discovered promise a better way of achieving goals? Does it simplify the path? Does it save time, money, or other resources? Then by all means, it should be pursued! However, if the technology doesn't relate to the library's goals, it can be a powerful and unwelcome deterrent.

The technology market has a way of presenting bright, shiny objects that grab attention. Some of these "shiny objects" (including devices, services, and more) deserve a closer look, while others do not. Testing the shiny against plan goals and objectives is a powerful way to decide.

Here's one example: let's say the technology plan calls for the library to use new social media approaches to connect with patrons. When this social media project was weighed against other pressing needs, it was decided early in the planning process that the library would not create its own social media site due to a lack of in-house technical expertise to build and administer a server. In addition, it was determined that the social media project was not a top priority at which to throw a lot of new resources—so it was decided to outsource the service to a vendor. In the process of vendor shopping, a new discovery is made: a free, open-source software program called "Ye Olde Liberry Facebooke" (or YOLF) that looks like it can do everything needed and more! The online demo of

YOLF is too cool for words—it makes the "other" Facebook look like a silly toy. But it has a catch: the vendor is providing source code (for free!), but it's up to users to make it run (hmm—it runs on something the creators call Linux/Apache/MySQL/PHP or LAMP). The creators offer support options—for free through online forums (where users ask questions, which can be answered by the software authors or other users) or for a small fee. Should this opportunity be pursued?

By this point in the book, my answer to the question is probably no surprise. Based on our hypothetical library's circumstances, YOLF is not only an awkward acronym, but it may also be impossible for the library to properly implement. It requires a good amount of tech know-how, time, and plain hard work to get it going—all things the library does not have. Plus—no matter how good it looks—why would any library try to launch its own social media site when there are so many other great ones it could simply join and participate in to meet the goal of using new approaches to social media to connect with patrons?

This example may seem silly, but I continue to be surprised at just how often similar situations arise in libraries, whether it's a library trying to chase the latest tech trend without considering how it helps or hinders its vision and goals or "commodity" technologies (including social media, but so many others) that are unnecessarily remade in a "library" version.

THE TYRANNY OF THE URGENT

Part of the job in information technology disciplines is responding to emerging and urgent needs. Despite best-laid plans, service responses requiring urgent attention are often at odds with the often more strategic needs addressed in a technology plan, resulting in plan items getting "kicked up the road" with the intention of addressing later. It's an ongoing battle. Most of the daily, urgent needs are legitimate, but some are unnecessary. Here are some things folks in IT departments in libraries across the United States may hear or experience:

- "I know you're really busy right now," she said, "but I need you to help with technology specs and budget for this really great grant I just found out about. To make the outreach part work, we're going to need something called a wireless service delivery infrastructure with built-in redundancy, whatever that is. Since you make everything look easy, I'm sure this is cake—maybe Google it? Anyway, we better get crackin'. The deadline is tomorrow!"
- "I don't really understand what you do in IT," he said on the same day the IT department was fighting a major system outage, "but can't you just buy and install this print management software? The website says it has a free trial download. Patron demands are killing us. My friends at the Schellbyville Library use it and it always works perfectly. I think."
- An IT worker walks in on a Monday with an already-full schedule for the day, including deadline tasks for several major technology plan projects. In the early morning hours, critical software security patches are released that need to be installed immediately—and one by one—on every computer in the library. The task will take at least four hours.

The day-to-day in any good technology shop is a constant exercise in evaluating, re-evaluating, and juggling priorities. A significant part of the job is being reactive to the unforeseen needs of the day, but unless some thought is given to the proactive pieces, the day can be filled responding to requests while the technology plan withers on the vine.

While this can often feel like an endless trap, it doesn't have to be. With a little mental fortitude and conviction, balance is possible. In facing the tyranny of the urgent, I believe there are two facts of technological life in the library:

1. If the library has created a technology plan, it has some obligation to at least attempt to complete it.
2. Every day something new will come up—begging for attention like a Labrador Retriever who sees a tennis ball just sitting on top of a desk . . .

For some reason, the new (exciting or maddening—depending on the situation) possibilities offered by number 2 have a way of demanding the lion's share of attention. It's easy to lose sight of the plan, so one strategy is to simply not let it get out of your sight.

- Post the plan—or perhaps just the current plan goals and tasks— to an office wall or whiteboard. Place it anywhere it can be seen regularly. Tape it to the front of a computer monitor every night so that it's the first thing seen when coming in to work in the morning. Put it in a place where it can serve as a reminder of all of the time spent creating it and all of the exciting, tangible possibilities it represents!
- Schedule a regular review of the elements. The technology plan doesn't just have a list of things to do—it also defined deadlines for completion, review, and progress reports. Try scheduling some special time monthly to do nothing but reread the plan. Use a personal schedule or calendar to devote to work on specific tasks (in advance of your deadlines, of course). The plan undoubtedly involves other people—why not invite them to help review parts of the plan?
- Commit to writing and sharing progress reports on a regular basis. Deadlines are wonderful, horrible things. They remind us of previous commitments that were so important at the time that we gave them special attention. Deadlines don't care what's happened in the meantime. Set some deadlines related to reporting

on plan progress—quarterly reports to the library board, a regular progress blog, a regular agenda item on team meetings—whatever would work to put a little appropriate pressure on keeping the plan moving forward.

- Doing these things puts the plan on the same footing as the emerging needs of the day, where they all get to battle it out for top priority!

Chapter Six

Evaluation of Library Technology

This chapter explores different methods that can be used to effectively evaluate library technology efforts and actions over time—including the technology plan but also the day-to-day and a look at strategies for course corrections in the likely chance of things changing over time! Evaluation is a straight-and-true arrow in the quiver of any library or technology manager. Somehow it must all work out, and somehow it can.

The major topics in this chapter include:

- what gets measured gets done (or at least the most attention)
- important things to measure
- approaches to measurement
- the "stop doing" list
- skill development: total cost of ownership (TCO)
- skill development: return on investment (ROI)
- things change: methods of course correction
- addictive statistics

WHAT GETS MEASURED GETS DONE (OR AT LEAST GETS THE MOST ATTENTION)

Regularly measuring the effectiveness of efforts is a robust method to ensure that the right things get priority attention. Many have heard the quote "What gets measured gets done." In other words, when a person is accountable to monitor an effort or activity—and record and report the results—it is more likely to actually happen. Although now a cliché in the business world, the idea of "what gets measured gets done" is sometimes a new concept in governmental institutions, including libraries. Earlier in this book, I suggested that technology plans should include a schedule to review and report progress. That's putting this concept into action!

Just measuring something has a powerful influence on whether—and how—an effort is executed. For instance, some technology plans will include a goal of attaining a particular degree of customer satisfaction such as this: "Within three years, our goal is for 90 percent of our in-house computer users to rate our computing resources as very good or excellent." Let's suppose for a moment that in year one of the plan, only 50 percent of library customers surveyed rated computing resources as "very good" or "excellent." In such an instance, I believe most libraries would immediately try to learn more about the cause of the low rating by asking fundamental questions such as:

- Are the computers too old or too slow?
- Does the Internet connection perform poorly?
- Are the monitors too small?
- Are the applications failing to meet user needs?
- Are the computers physically difficult to use?
- Is the seating uncomfortable?

Based on the cause of patron dissatisfaction, most libraries would address the concerns to improve the patron's computing experience—and in the course hopefully receive higher satisfaction ratings in the next survey.

Of course, just measuring something doesn't mean it will always get done. But measuring is a good strategy to ensure that the most important things also get the most attention, especially as emerging needs and downright surprises fight for daily attention.

Measurements come in all shapes and sizes—from objective efforts such as formal data collection and analysis, subjective "gut" responses, and all points in between. In this chapter, we'll focus mostly on the objective approach, but sometimes measures and responses can be quick and decisive. Recently, in a class I teach on essential hardware and software in libraries, I was working with students on the process of keeping computer workstations clean, especially public computers that experience a lot of use in a given day—and in due course tend to be a collection point for dirt and grime. A student asked, "How often should we clean our public computers?" My answer was "Take a look at the workstation and ask yourself if you would feel comfortable sitting there and using it. If the answer is no, it's time to clean it!"

WHAT ARE THE MOST IMPORTANT THINGS TO MEASURE?

One nice thing about technology is it often comes with built-in ways to measure the things that it does. For instance, I'm writing this using a word processor that allows me at any time to pull up statistics about the document I'm working on, including word count, which is one of the stats to consider regarding optimum size for a chapter of this type. That same report (in Microsoft Word, it's found in File > Properties) can also tell me how long I've been working on this page, the data size of the file, and more. This feature is a simple example that shows that collecting and reporting data is at the core of many computer operations—and also is often overlooked as we try to improve approaches and processes.

That brings to mind the question of what is useful to measure—and what is not. Just because something is passively measured and reported by a software application—such as the word count on this document—does not necessarily mean that it's valuable. In fact, with so much data available, it's a likely possibility that most of us already feel buried in minutiae.

Big data companies like Google seem to take the approach of "collect it all and sort it out later." And for Google that makes sense—it's their businesses, and they are wired for the collection, accumulation, and harvesting of what is known as "big data." And although I think libraries should be collecting and reporting more data than most currently do (with the purpose of guiding service and operational decisions), I also believe all library data collected and communicated should have a purpose.

A trap libraries can fall in regarding data collection relates to patron confidentiality. In both library culture and library law, libraries are charged to do more than most entities in protecting the confidentiality of patron data. At the same time, many libraries are not equipped to technologically ensure those protections. In other words, hearts are in the right place, but the actual security capabilities, skills, and practices may not be sufficient to live up to the goal of confidentiality. At the same time, patrons are expecting more services that (sometimes unbeknownst to them) are highly dependent on the collection of personal data. What to do? Many libraries simply choose to collect as little patron data as possible, which helps serve the confidentiality issue but doesn't help provide more data-driven services to patrons. This is an important and sensitive topic (and outside the scope of this book) that I believe will emerge as one of the key issues libraries will face in the coming years.

Every library may answer the "what to measure" question a little differently, but there are safe bets with which to start. One critical area is any basic requirements as tied to annual reports, grants, surveys, or documents such as the library's long-range or strategic plan or the technology plan.

If you're a library director or manager, you are probably already familiar with measures that you submit as part of annual surveys but may not be aware of all of the statistical gathering places in library land. A few to sample are below, but keep searching for more if you don't find one that addresses your exact area of interest.

Readings on the topic: Statistics

- **Public Library Data Service and PLAmetrics** (http://www.ala.org/pla/publications/plds): This essential comparison of library statistics—available in both print and electronic versions—provides comparative stats in the areas of technology, finance, library use, and others from more than 1,100 libraries in the United States and Canada.
- **ALA Office for Research and Evaluation** (http://www.ala.org/offices/ors): From the ALA website: "The mission of the Office for Research and Statistics (ORS) is to provide leadership and expert advice to ALA staff, members and public on all matters related to research and statistics about libraries, librarians and other library staff; represent the Association to Federal agencies on these issues; and initiate projects needed to expand the knowledge base of the field through research and the collection of useful statistics."
- **Library Research Service** (http://www.lrs.org): The Colorado-based Library Research Service (a unit of the Colorado State Library) provides library-centered research in many formats, including its popular "Fast Facts" and "Closer Look" series. Not just centered on Colorado issues, the site format and connection to national data make it a relevant

and interesting stop, especially the report on the impact of
school librarians on student achievement. LRS also has
created RIPL (Research Institute for Public Libraries),
which hosts national and regional library data summits,
teaching participants techniques in data gathering and analysis. RIPL website: https://ripl.lrs.org/.

- **Pew Internet and American Life Project** (http://www.
  pewinternet.org/): Funded by the Pew Charitable Trust (and
  one of seven Pew Research Center projects), the Pew Internet and Life Project conducts and publishes studies exploring the impact of the Internet on people and society. From
  the mission statement: "The Project produces reports exploring the impact of the Internet on families, communities,
  work and home, daily life, education, health care, and civic
  and political life." Recent studies have centered on broadband use, social networking, the digital divide, and other
  vital topics. The formal reports are easy, compelling reads,
  and those who like to run their own numbers can download
  the raw data collected for each survey.

- **Edge Assessment** (http://www.libraryedge.org/): This for-
  pay service was created by a cross section of national library organizations to help create comparative metrics for
  public library technological effectiveness. From the Edge
  website: "Edge helps public libraries better serve their communities though improved public technology services. The
  Edge Toolkit is based on a national set of benchmarks for
  public libraries to evaluate their technology services, and
  includes resources, recommendations, and tools for strategic planning and community engagement."

- **Project Outcome** (https://www.projectoutcome.org/):
  From the Project Outcome website: "Project Outcome is a
  free toolkit designed to help public libraries understand and
  share the true impact of essential library services and pro-

grams by providing simple surveys and an easy-to-use process for measuring and analyzing outcomes. Project Outcome also provides libraries with the resources and training support needed to apply their results and confidently advocate for their library's future."

MEASURES RELATED TO YOUR TECHNOLOGY

Whether they are required by surveys or not, several technology measures can be used to help understand how library resources are used—and that also can be used to make strategic decisions.

One excellent measure is customer satisfaction with overall technology efforts or some particular area that may require special attention. In most libraries, there are at least two distinct customer groups for technology efforts (patrons and staff) with each having different needs. When asking the satisfaction questions, it's important to ask each group the question separately.

Since data collection and comparison require resources (including staff time and cash), it's important to hone in on what measures are the most important and then consistently perform those measures over time to provide comparative data. Data by itself is just a snapshot in time, but data collected consistently over a span of time can be a powerful and insightful tool that can identify trends and be used to understand the past and present and to help make decisions about the future.

Activity: we are increasingly a data-driven society, and libraries are increasingly enjoying the benefits of data collection and analysis. If you haven't yet stepped into those waters, it's time for you to start. Look at the list in the textbox and pick at least three to start. If you're already there, I would challenge you to look at what you're routinely measuring and ask whether the efforts are delivering what you most need or if you need to consider different measures.

There are other basics that are helpful to know—here are a few that you may already measure. If not, you should consider adding them to your annual tally.

- number of items circulated every year
- number of active patrons registered
- number of hours patron computers are in use (or number of user sessions)
- number of users of your wireless systems
- number of annual page views of your website or specific web pages
- number of searches performed annually within your ILS
- use (in number of searches or number of documents accessed) of subscription databases
- anything useful you can imagine

OPTIONS TO MEASURE TECHNOLOGICAL EFFECTIVENESS

It's time to do some digging. What options are available as part of the existing technology systems in the library? For instance, all ILS systems provide some level of valuable statistical reporting. Some of the methods are less than perfect (some systems, for instance, can only archive several weeks of particular data measures), but nonetheless, they are there—and with the proper discipline, gathering the stats can be a powerful resource. Some providers of web services, such as web hosts and subscription database vendors, have basic measurements built in as part of their services.

Even though some systems only provide raw numbers and not graphical views, there are ways to create charts and graphs of raw data. Spreadsheet programs like Microsoft Excel and Google Sheets have the capability to turn rows of numbers into charts and graphs—just use the help menu of your program to look up "charts" and give it a whirl. If data collection needs are simple or when trying to collect and report stats on a shoestring, this approach provides a nice quick-start.

Simple surveys—through tick sheets, paper surveys, or electronic methods—are another handy way to gather information. Doing what's called a statistically valid survey is best left to the experts, but don't let that be a barrier from the worthy activity of asking users simple questions about their feelings and experiences with your technology.

THE "STOP DOING" LIST

Other than the things that are counted, lots of other things get done in a typical library. What should continue and—more importantly—what should give?

If there is one characteristic folks working in libraries tend to share, it's the sincere desire to help others. It's a beautiful quality, and I believe it's one of the reasons the public continues to hold libraries in such high esteem. The willingness of librarians and other library workers to go above and beyond is not the exception but the norm.

There's a trap, though, in trying to do everything for everyone or—from an institutional perspective—be everything to everyone. With the best intentions, many try. But I believe it's an unattainable goal. Most libraries have limited resources, including people power and budget. When adding something new, it's reasonable to expect that something else should stop. Simply put, something has to give.

The daily re-prioritization that goes on in any IT shop is indeed an ongoing effort—the high-priority tasks get attention, and the low-priority tasks shuffle to the bottom, perhaps never to be considered worthy of effort again.

There is a trick to this, though—all re-prioritization should be a conscious decision, made in consultation with others (as appropriate), and monitored and reported like any other activity. Not only is it important for others in your organization to understand your re-prioritization decisions (and perhaps even have an opportunity to challenge them), but it will be good for you to have a personal bread-crumb trail later to help you remember why some efforts lost over time.

DETERMINING THE TOTAL
COST OF OWNERSHIP (TCO)

One of the first questions that comes up when considering a technology expense is "How much is this going to cost?" It's a good question: technology investments are often expensive, in particular on the "front end"—that is, when introducing an entirely new thing or system to the library. Many of us have even experienced a situation where the final costs of a technology effort went far beyond original expectations. Ouch!

The best way to avoid such an unpleasant surprise is to estimate the total cost of ownership—or TCO—of the effort. When estimating TCO, any vendor quotes are simply the starting point (and solely relying on vendor's estimates often leads to unexpected cost overruns later). Vendors often do their best to give you accurate costs, but it's difficult for them to know all of the elements faced on the journey to the bottom line.

There is no one way to determine TCO, but here are a few factors that should be considered:

- research (including creation of "requests for proposals" or "requests for information")
- vendor quotes (may include some of the items below)
- hardware
- software
- new processes (including security, backup and restore, etc.)

- installation (including any retro-conversion or migration expenses)
- training
- ongoing support (including warrantees, annual maintenance contracts, etc.)
- licensing
- insurance
- construction costs
- any new labor costs (including project management, IT staff time, testing, etc.)
- any downtime due to transition
- replacement costs (over time—expected lifetime of initial investment)
- any other long-term expenses

Let's take this concept out for a run. The worksheet (offering a very simplified look at TCO) can be used to review any project that has already been completed—just fill in the blanks! In the Management of Technology class that I teach, the bottom line often surprises students, followed by students applying the concept of TCO to many other areas of effort and expense!

RETURN ON INVESTMENT

TCO exercises often result in an acute case of sticker shock. Yikes! This is going to cost how much!?

But the dollars tell only part of the story—I believe the most important factor is not the cost but the value. So how can we determine if a proposed project or effort offers a high enough value to proceed? A return on investment (or ROI) exercise can help provide the answer.

A classic ROI analysis is often applied to financial investments and helps determine the real or projected profitability of the dollars invested over a given period of time. When we look at ROI in

Purchase our own folder/sealer

TCO:

	One Time Cost	Ongoing Costs (annually)	Total (year 1)	Total (year 2)	Total (year 3)	Total (Year 4)	Total (year 5)
Folder/Sealer (w/5 year warranty)	3,500.00	$0.00	$11,250.00	$19,000.00	$26,750.00	$34,500.00	$42,250.00
Paper Forms	0.00	$500.00					
Toner	0.00	$200.00					
Postage	0.00	$5,000.00					
Power for Unit	0.00	$50.00					
Staff Labor	0.00	$2,000.00					
totals	3,500.00	$7,750.00					

ROI:

			Total (year 1)	Total (year 2)	Total (year 3)	Total (Year 4)	Total (year 5)
Staff Labor Savings			$2,000.00	$4,000.00	$6,000.00	$8,000.00	$10,000.00
ROI			$1,999.00	$3,999.00	$5,999.00	$7,999.00	$9,999.00

Outsource disc notice printing

	One Time Cost	Ongoing Costs (annually)	Total (year 1)	Total (year 2)	Total (year 3)	Total (Year 4)	Total (year 5)
Joe's Print Shack (5 year price lock)	$0.00	$3,000.00	$9,000.00	$18,000.00	$27,000.00	$36,000.00	$45,000.00
Paper Forms	$0.00	$0.00					
Toner	$0.00	$0.00					
Postage		$5,000.00					
Power for Unit	$0.00	$0.00					
Staff Labor	$0.00	$1,000.00					
totals	$0.00	$9,000.00					

ROI:

			Total (year 1)	Total (year 2)	Total (year 3)	Total (Year 4)	Total (year 5)
Staff Labor Savings			$3,000.00	$6,000.00	$9,000.00	$12,000.00	$15,000.00
ROI			$2,999.00	$5,999.00	$8,999.00	$11,999.00	$14,999.00

Figure 6.1. Purchase vs. Outsource Printing

libraries, we don't usually expect to make a profit in dollars. There are some exceptions (for instance, the ROI of using e-commerce to collect library fines online or adding an automated pay-for-print system might result in new or increased revenue for the library), but generally the "return" for most of us will be in terms of greater efficiencies, higher levels of customer service, or getting more per-formance-per-dollar invested using one approach versus another.

One way to look at ROI in libraries is regarding greater staff efficiencies. If the library is experiencing greater demand (such as higher circulation) but can't afford to increase the size of staff (an expense that often tends to be enduring), technologies such as self-service, RFID (Radio Frequency Identification), or Automated Ma-terials Handling (AMH) are often considered to meet patron de-mand without increasing staff. In this case, the return on investment can be measured by comparing the cost of the project (using TCO) to the cost of hiring additional staff and projecting the effectiveness of both approaches. As with TCO, ROI can be used to compare the financial differences between leasing equipment and buying it out-right.

As well, ROI can be used to compare several different approaches to solving problems. For instance, let's compare buying pre-made self-check units from a vendor versus building them using off-the-shelf parts. When I worked at the Fort Collins Public Library, we did that very study—and due to our unique factors (including a highly skilled and willing IT department), we determined that for about the same amount of dollars we could build many more ourselves compared to buying pre-made self-checks. As well, we felt confident that servicing the units—and keeping them operating and functional—would be much easier than our past experiences with a vendor.

Time proved that we made an excellent choice—and one based on our particular situation. This certainly would not be the case for all libraries—by understanding our objectives and studying our unique circumstances, we came to the "build" conclusion. If we didn't have a strong IT department or didn't have a demand for more points of self-service, our ROI study could have lead to a very different conclusion.

As daunting as a good TCO study can be, a good ROI can be even more nuanced. Let's try a simple approach to help illustrate the most important points.

Amanda is the director of a midsized library in Anytown, USA. After she had taken my class, she decided to create her technology plan, and one of the tasks (to support a high-level goal of using technology to create better staff efficiencies) was to buy a printer/sealer for circulation notices (instead of asking staff to hand-fold them). The task seemed pretty straightforward at first, but now she's not so sure. She checked the cost (a whopping $3,500) and felt a little sticker shock. On a whim, she called a local printer who offered to print all of her circ notices daily for $3,000 per year.

What to Do?

She had often heard vendors tout the concept of "return on investment"—and thought perhaps that could help with her dilemma. Amanda worked with her business librarian to define "return on investment" and found that the simplest definition came from the world of finance, essentially a formula that looks like this

ROI = (Gain from Investment - Cost of Investment)/Cost of Investment

In her research, she also learned that many others (especially those in nonprofit agencies or undertaking amorphous things like showing the value of a social media campaign) used the basics of the ROI formula to help make decisions. Like the others, *the point wasn't to return a profit*, but to see if her potential investment might *"pay for itself"* over time versus other options.

Amanda knew the only way it possibly could *"pay for itself"* is if the new machine—or outsourcing option—also saved staff time (measured in the cost of labor). Amanda worked with her circ department and determined that the machine would cut in half the amount of staff time to create notices, while outsourcing the printing would cut it by 75 percent.

Here's how Amanda compared the cost of each approach—and also used TCO to gauge the costs with a high level of accuracy.

Figure 6.2.   ROI illustration

- Amanda was amazed to see the how the numbers played out over time (she had never given much thought to how much it cost to perform this seemingly simple function).
- Even though the TCO for buying a folder/sealer was lower than outsourcing over a five-year period, the ROI was drastically different!
- Amanda realized that the ROI numbers wouldn't result in real cash, but as her circ department has gotten increasingly busy, she could see how outsourcing this function could free up staff time for other demands.

Review Amanda's References

http://en.wikipedia.org/wiki/Return_on_investment
http://en.wikipedia.org/wiki/Application_portfolio_
   management#Return_on_Investment

THINGS CHANGE: METHODS OF COURSE CORRECTION FOR TECHNOLOGY EFFORTS

What happens when things aren't going as planned? There are at least two choices (other than lying down quietly and hoping the problem will go away): change your course or change your goal.

Changing or modifying your goal is a legitimate technique, although hopefully a very rare one. Everyone has bitten off more than a chewable portion at one time or another, came to a new understanding of an effort, or (often in the case of technology) discovered that what seemed like an excellent idea or approach has become irrelevant or obsolete. When taking the healthy first step of writing a goal and communicating it to others, it's equally important to do the same for any goals that are changed, modified, or eliminated. One caution—if goals are changing frequently, then the goal-setting approach is probably flawed, and it's time to rethink how the goals were created to begin with.

Table 6.1.   Simple TCO Worksheet—Library IT

Expense	Amount
Staff time—research	$0.00
Vendor quote	$0.00
Hardware	$0.00
Software	$0.00
Installation (not covered by vendor quote)	$0.00
Training (not covered by vendor quote)	$0.00
Ongoing support (i.e., maintenance contracts)	$0.00
Licensing	$0.00
Insurance	$0.00
Construction costs	$0.00
Labor costs (incl. project management)	$0.00
Total	$0.00

(It's ok to use rough estimates—if you don't know, leave amount blank.)

More often, though, simple course corrections are more appropriate, especially in considering the tasks performed in pursuit of the goals. For instance, in the case of a goal of "high patron satisfaction with public computers," a library may survey users and discover that they're not very happy with the old, slow computers that they have available to them. So new computers are purchased in the hope that customer satisfaction will improve. But what happens if the next survey shows that patrons are still unhappy? The goal needn't change (it's pretty good), but a little more work should be done to find the cause of patron dissatisfaction. Is the Internet too slow? Is needed software missing? Is there some other issue? Digging deeper will suggest new options to help meet the goal.

ADDICTIVE STATS

As any baseball fan can tell you, statistics are addictive. If a library is already using something like Google Analytics to collect and analyze website data or if library managers and staff are enamored by the info-graphics that can be seen daily online (or monthly in periodicals such as *Wired* magazine) or even are fascinated by the action the library gets on social media, then those involved may be considered a "dataholic." And in our interconnected and constantly measured world, I'm not sure that there is—or if there should be—a cure. Good data collection and analysis can help libraries greatly as they chart their course in the modern world.

A word of warning, though: data collection can be so attractive that it can be an end unto itself. Since data collection of any kind requires resources (sometimes significant resources), proceed cautiously. Data helps libraries, and hopefully, we are data-driven. But for most public libraries, the core "business" is public service—I believe we connect people to information at no direct cost as a public Good (capital G, indeed). Libraries can measure whether technology goals have been achieved, the number of times people have been served with technology resources, and even how satisfied patrons are with library technology, but other areas don't easily lend themselves to the cold, hard light of statistics. I believe libraries—often very subtly and privately—significantly improve the quality of life for our communities. I'm not sure it will ever be possible to measure those intangible, essential elements in a form other than anecdotal—through the telling and retelling of great stories.

Chapter Seven

Advanced Topics and Putting It All Together

As simple as the fundamentals of technology can be, even a book such as this one about the basics of tech management should address some of the "next-level" issues. These are topics that often emerge in the form of questions like "But what about . . . ?" as we dive into technology subjects.

In Part 1: Advanced Topics of this chapter we address:

- disruptive technologies and their value
- the importance of understanding the "why" behind others' technology actions
- cycles of success and failure
- strategies for correcting course on budgets
- people skills
- computer and data security

As in chapter 1, it might be helpful to think of these topics as "bite-sized" looks at relevant topics in technology management that don't fit easily into a single category but help provide a framework to understand and evaluate technology in general.

As well, we recap some of the core concepts in this book in Part 2: Putting It All Together.

PART 1: ADVANCED TOPICS

Disruptive Technologies and Their Value

Some technologies emerge that are transparent—while they may be very helpful, their visible impact is minimal. In libraries, we often see these as refinements to existing technologies (such as the improvements brought to our library automation systems and other software via new releases or a slightly different or more efficient layout to a website).

Disruptive technologies are a whole different thing and can be described as a new something that changes everything—hopefully in a good way but not always and rarely in a black-or-white fashion. The Internet itself is a great example, drastically changing libraries (and almost everything else, for that matter), but there are others throughout history more closely related to libraries, such as:

- library automation systems (disrupting the card catalog)
- subscription databases (disrupting print reference materials)
- Radio Frequency Identification (RFID) for physical materials (augmenting and disrupting barcode-only tracking systems)
- and many more

In each of those examples, an old way of doing things was disrupted by a new way—and the new way brought with it methods, options, and possibilities unavailable before.

Many of us are so used to the paradigm and consistent introduction of disruptive technologies that we're a bit underwhelmed when it doesn't happen with a big bang. The introduction of Apple's iPad in 2010 is a good example—at the time (and before its release), some were expecting it to have a slate of far-fetched futuristic features and were initially disappointed that it was essentially a larger version of the company's palm-sized iPod touch. But was the iPad, with its larger size; integrated eBook reader; access to multiple sources of media; thousands of popular, mature software applications; and integrated store disruptive? Indeed, yes.

The value of disruptive technologies is not just how they can make existing processes or tasks better or more efficient, but how they can change many things—hopefully for the better—and all at once.

Today, our implementation tasks are less about encountering disruptive technologies one by one and more about choosing which ones to pursue and managing/balancing the ones in our technology stables.

Never Copy the "What" Without Understanding the "Why"

Models are great, and the successful outcomes, results, and products of others can make wonderful targets for our own efforts. Additionally, it's very healthy to ask the question "What are other libraries doing in this new area the library is interested in exploring?" But none of those things are more important than the "why" behind the visible result.

Technology is all about options. There are most often multiple ways to select and use technology to solve a problem, and often, within single technological solutions, there are dizzying arrays of options to mold and deploy it. The best implementations of technology support clear goals and objectives (as covered in a previous chapter). When looking at what others choose, I always try to ask the "why" question to understand their choice. In the process, it's often discovered that another's goals, objectives—and especially circumstances—are very different than mine. And in asking the question, it may be discovered that this is the first time that this vital information has ever really been articulated by our hero library!

My favorite example is when our library management team, looking for inspiration for a new construction project, visited a progressive library renowned for its excellent designs, customer service, and leading-edge approach to librarianship. During the tours, I noticed some curious choices in the way certain technologies (patron computers, RFID, self-checkout, and automated materials handling) were configured and deployed. These choices were so distinct from others I had seen that I had to know more. I pulled the director aside and asked questions about his objectives. As it turned out, the choices made for the technological configurations (as well as many other aspects of their functional design) were designed to support the data collection measures needed to reflect the library's rising circulation. The data would further support the director's rationale for a funding increase in an upcoming election. In light of that driver, everything that I previously thought odd made perfect sense! Assume nothing. Always ask the "why" question!

Cycles of Success, Cycles of Failure

Of course, not everything goes as planned. In terms of technology, it's a given that things sometimes will not work. There are systems—those considered "mission critical" like the ILS and network—that require constant and priority attention to ensure functionality and uptime. There are others, though, that benefit from flexibility—and even failure on the road to ultimate success.

The idea of "failing to succeed" might be a new one in the library world, but it's common in so many others. Library workers of all stripes tend to hold themselves to the highest standards, and wanting to do a good job is indeed among the most admirable of qualities. The idea of failure of any kind can seem beyond distasteful. In technology efforts, testing and piloting approaches—especially before making them "live" (when staff and patrons are depending on the services or devices)—is a best practice that is not followed often enough. A good pilot project is an excellent way to test things, fail behind the scenes, make improvements, and ensure things are working before people and processes depend on the technology.

When working with technology, failure is part of the cycle of success. Try, learn, grow—and ultimately succeed!

Things Change: Methods of Course Correction for Budgets

Technology can be expensive, but library managers needn't live in fear of what the next big budgetary hit might be. Here are some budget strategies that can help.

Many libraries have an annual budget process, but some are on a two-year budget cycle. Those having a biennial budget already know how tough it is to provide for technology expenses. Most library managers start preparing budgets at least six months in advance of the next fiscal year, which adds even more time to the guesses made in trying to provide for the often-volatile world of technology. Even for annual budgets, eighteen months is a long time when considering tech expenses.

Here's an easy way to make sure you have enough funds to keep technology going strong and to be able to handle any new things that might be needed between budget cycles.

It can be helpful to think of a technology budget in three broad chunks:

- maintenance—keeping current stuff going
- growth—providing for new stuff that can be foreseen
- innovation—providing for new stuff that can't yet be foreseen but will be needed nonetheless

Maintenance dollars are important but often overlooked. For instance, what do many technology managers think of when the state library announces that the library has been awarded twenty brand-new public workstations? When this happened to me, the first thing I felt was gratitude, followed by planning and budgeting to maintain those computers and further creating a plan to replace them when the inevitable happens and they reach the end of their useful life in several years. Just making them available in turn creates a new level of expectation from patrons. Other areas require equal attention. Most libraries are reliant on their networks—and to ensure that they function, it's essential to budget for maintenance and support of switches, WiFi access points, and other equipment. All technology has a useful life and during that time requires maintenance dollars and efforts.

Growth dollars are for all of those projects on the technology plan and often take the form of mini-budgets for each area of effort. When budgeting for these projects, it's important to include appropriate contingency dollars (usually 5 to 10 percent of certain lines or the entire budget) depending on how confident the manager is concerning the costs, the environment, and the library's situation. Most projects include a surprise or two, and I've found that to deliver projects as inexpensively as possible, some managers fail to include contingency dollars—leading to disaster when a snag comes up. With good project management and a little luck, contingency funds may never need to be touched at all—and those dollars can be returned to the technology or general library budget for other uses.

Innovation dollars are another overlooked need. I might not know what incredibly great things might emerge in the next two years, but I do know that there will be some yet unknown incredibly great things that I will, in turn, greatly desire. Ideally, some funds should be made available to invest in new and unforeseen innovation, but most often (and despite the inevitable nature of technological advancement) not much thought is given to this area in library technology budgets. This can be provided for in several ways—either through earmarking reserves or being ultra-thrifty to save funds as we go in other areas to use for innovative needs—so I hope to see more libraries providing for innovation funds over time.

People Skills (for Managers)

While I hope every leader's and manager's people skills are excellent, what I mean here are the personal drivers and skills of the people helping lead and maintain library technology efforts.

Many of us feel that it is passion (for helping others, for connecting people to information, for being an integral part of a public Good) and not money that brings folks into the library field. In terms of IT workers, this statement may ring even louder. When it comes to pay, library IT is not at the top of any scales that I'm aware of.

As a manager or director, it's crucial that you understand why your IT people are with you, what skills they bring to the table, and how you can help them. As in the assessment chapter, it's time to take another inventory of some of the softer skills that your IT people possess.

Why are they working in library IT? Do they love the profession like I've inferred? Are they just picking up a paycheck? Somewhere in between?

What areas of expertise do they have? No matter how simple or grand your IT efforts are, start with the question "Is the work getting done?" Next, look at the individual skill sets of staff—is the library heavy in any one area of expertise and light in others? What areas are most needed? Are there gaps?

Most directors and managers are aware of the power of coaching and probably already do it quite a bit with staff members who share their areas of expertise. Even those without an IT background should coach their IT workers, too!

Do the library's IT workers come from a traditional IT background? If so, the IT staff might benefit from an understanding of the public service role of the library. Folks from a strict IT background might not be aware of vital library concerns such as the importance of patron privacy and confidentiality, public service, intuitive systems and services, friendly technology, and more. Folks from an IT background tend to value clear objectives and processes—if you can elevate library values to objective status, it's likely you will be delighted at how they can use technology to address the challenges of a library. How can these folks be helped to better understand and support library culture?

Do library IT workers come from a library background? If the library IT staff is composed of librarians who were promoted after showing an interest or aptitude in technology, they need a different sort of coaching. They might need some support in IT training (managing and administering specific platforms and technologies), IT culture, industry trends, and more. How can you help these folks dive deeper into the IT pool?

Do they have training and/or culture in both IT and libraries? Give 'em a raise and all the resources they need to propel your institutions to greatness! These people are rare yet essential to modern libraries.

This "soft skills" inventory doesn't stop with people on the payroll. Some libraries outsource some or all of the people needed to run their systems. Do outsourcers understand libraries? Do they support the public service mission of the library, or are some of their solutions at odds with library needs? Are the library and the outsourcer able to communicate with each other in plain language?

Computer and Data Security

Many of us who manage technology efforts can't help but be concerned every time there is news of an electronic security breach, and what risks might be present at the library? The concern is justified. Libraries do not tend to be big targets for hackers and crackers, but libraries do collect personal data and serve many patrons with computer access. By statute and by culture, libraries protect patron confidentiality. Libraries have a responsibility to protect patrons from external cyber threats and also from each other.

Security can be complicated, but one concept can help guide your approach: security is not something done one time but is an ongoing process. The best way to approach security is through multiple layers; it's not enough to buy an "Internet Security" software package to install on your PCs or servers and call it good.

The basics, however, are still important. If you don't have an "Internet Security" software package on every one of your Windows PCs functioning correctly and with up-to-date virus definitions, stop reading this now and take care of business. And if you don't know whether you do or not, your need to find out just became even more urgent.

On bigger systems, a data breach is always a risk. When it comes to library automation systems, one approach is to never collect more data from patrons than you absolutely need to do business. Regular and systematic backups of important data (as well as periodic testing to ensure that backed-up data is recoverable) should be a part of the daily routine in any library. Is that happening?

Computer security is a big topic—suffice to say that it's beyond the scope of this book. If you have an IT shop in your library, ask them about their approach to security. If not, get some outside help to evaluate your systems and make any necessary improvements.

PART 2: PUTTING IT ALL TOGETHER

This book covers a lot of ground—here's a brief recap of the main points.

Technology Vision

Your vision for technology is more important than any of the individual choices you may make to achieve your vision. Technology is all about options, and there are almost always multiple paths to any particular goal. The best path can be chosen based on a clear vision.

Regardless of your position in a library, but especially for directors and managers, your view of technology in both short and long terms has a cascading effect throughout your entire organization. From the polar extremes of the bleeding-edge advocate to the Luddite, your view will set the tone for what you do with technology and how it's accomplished.

Your staff and colleagues will expect your vision to change over time—and perhaps nothing in our lives changes faster than technology. But please don't forget how important it is to commit to and communicate your vision. If you have a good IT staff, your outlook on technology is very important to them, and they will aspire to meet your needs and expectations. It's your job to make sure they understand what those needs and expectations are!

Communicate early and often. Ask questions. Make it safe for subordinates to debate and otherwise test your ideas. Likewise, debate and test theirs. Good vision can be as simple as the results from good conversations.

Technology Management

To do a good job of managing your technology, remember to take the time to understand whom you serve, what you have, and what you want.

Understanding whom you serve can be as simple as dividing your people into two major groups (such as patrons and staff) or getting into the nitty-gritty of studying the demographics of library users, both in-house and via your electronic services. Starting simple is good because it helps you make broader decisions based on the greatest needs—and more granular data can help you focus on serving key groups in the most powerful manner possible.

Knowing what you have is an important next step. Choices (both conscious and unconscious) were made to build your inventory of electronic gear and services. Hopefully most of the choices were good, but some might have been poor. Creating an inventory, reviewing, and assessing is your base point for any changes. With any luck, you will be able to build on your existing strengths and shore up any weak areas.

Don't forget about the people who make your technology run—understanding their skills, strengths, and weaknesses can help you form productive teams.

Knowing what you want is guided by your vision. The sky is the limit, and your budget is the anchor. Most of us fall somewhere in between!

Technology Budget

In a sky-is-the-limit world of technology, I described your budget as an anchor. But hopefully it's also your engine—and in conjunction with staff your primary resource—to provide the best possible services for patrons and the best possible support for library staff.

Technology budgets are approached in different ways, but as with other activities, it's wise to first look at how you've spent in the past, compare with how you spend now, and spot the trends. With that information, you can look to the future to see what changes will deliver what you need in the most powerful and efficient manner possible.

Technology dollars can add up quickly—and it's just as easy to spend dollars on the frivolous as it is on the vital. One approach is to consider a return on investment (ROI) analysis to show how technological investment returns efficiencies—and/or dollars—to the organization. When viewed through that lens, projects thought to be expensive may appear to actually be a bargain. In turn, projects thought to be a bargain may actually be quite expensive.

One way to think about your technology budget is to break it down into large chunks—perhaps as a mix of ongoing costs (which you should evaluate annually); planned new costs (such as projects or new services); and innovation opportunities (monies set aside to allow you to strike while the iron is hot).

Technology Planning

We spent more time on technology planning in this book than in any other area. Tech planning often gets short shrift in libraries and is often only begrudgingly employed when absolutely necessary, such as part of a grant requirement. But technology has become more important than an afterthought—working its way into almost every aspect of library operations and functions. If we fail to plan our approach to technology, we create unnecessary peril and force ourselves into nonstop reactive mode.

It's understandable, though, why some are timid to approach technology planning. Simply put, it's a lot of work!

A good technology plan can give you several advantages, including targets for achievement and a way to evaluate new opportunities as they emerge. The time spent planning helps further hone your vision and approach and makes the work of evaluating the new much easier.

Technology Implementation

Staying on target when implementing technology can be as tough as public services. Every day is an exercise in understanding the priorities and adjusting as necessary. And it's so easy to get distracted.

There are many wonderful (and some not-so-wonderful) things that can distract you from your plans. Every day brings new surprises and challenges that warrant a response. New technologies can appear (both for you and for patrons) that have the potential of upsetting the whole apple cart. Good and not-so-good ideas can come from staff and patrons. The new hot thing could indeed be hot—or a dud.

Again, your technology plan is your first line of defense. By planning and committing to the plan, you provide yourself with something tangible against which to measure new efforts. It also presents the realities involved in the things you've committed to in terms of time, staff, money, and other resources. It's possible (and sometimes preferable) to change course, but it should always be done consciously. Having a plan makes it easier for those conscious moves to happen.

As well, good people and a clear budget are two approaches to deciding what—and when—to implement. A good team with the right diverse mix of styles can be a powerful factor in implementation, and a good budget can both be an engine for your efforts and an anchor to ensure that you stay within reasonable boundaries.

Evaluation of Technology

What gets measured gets done (or at least the most attention). Most of us find that this is a true statement, so take care to select good measures to drive your efforts and decisions. One approach is to center on the factors that are most important and do a good job of consistently measuring and comparing the results over time.

Lots of other things get done too, so it's wise to reassess and evaluate whether you should continue doing them. Your institutional plans, including technology, long range, or others, are powerful guideposts in the decision process. Libraries often try to do everything for everyone—but that comes at a cost.

The nuts and bolts of measuring your tech efforts can be simple or complex, depending on your needs. If you're new to this, start simple. If this is old hat, you probably dine on statistics each morning for breakfast!

Not only are stats interesting, but they also help you make decisions for course corrections over time, including how you deploy your human resources and spend your dollars.

Data collection for its own sake can be fun, but it also involves resources. Certainly measure what's important, but remember that each effort to gather stats equals the expenditure of resources, in terms of time or money.

SUMMARY AND CONCLUSION

While I believe there will always be a place for words and images to be printed on paper and bound together in wonderful volumes called books (for what they do, books are a near-perfect technology), information technology of an electronic nature is clearly the future of libraries. While the implications can be both good and bad, Pandora's box has been opened. The genie is out of the bottle. Insert your favorite cliché here!

Most of us would agree that Gutenberg's printing press was a technological advancement that allowed people everywhere to have unprecedented access to ideas and information, bringing with it the potential to make their lives richer. Is our electronic present—and future—really that much different?

It's not so much a matter of whether you're managing technology in your institutions but how you're approaching it. Often it's considered an add-on or something outside of regular library services. I hope over the course of this book, you have seen how technology is integrated within your own library and perhaps now have a new vision for what you want to do with this powerful resource.

Index

About the Author

Carson Block has been a library technologist for twenty years—as a library worker, IT director, and now library technology consultant. His passions include leading technology visioning, planning, and other activities designed to help build the library's capacity to serve communities. As a consultant, Carson is often brought in to help solve complex institutional issues and to help align the library's public service mission with its technology efforts to serve the needs of patrons and staff.

Carson is a director-at-large for the American Library Association's Association of Special and Cooperative Library Agencies (ASCLA) and is a past chair of ASCLA's Library Consultant's Interest Group. He is also a member of the Future of Libraries advisory group to ALA's Office of Information Technology Policy and a member of the former Twenty-first Century Libraries Committee of ALA's Office of Information Technology Policy (OITP). Carson is also past president of the Colorado Division of the Public Library Association. Carson continues to advocate for libraries through many activities, including facilitating a group of librarians (called lib*interactive) engaging the technology, film, and music communities at the SXSW conference.

Made in the USA
San Bernardino, CA
15 August 2017